ASSASSIN'S CREED

VALHALLA

ILLUSTRATION BY DOUGLAS P. LOBO

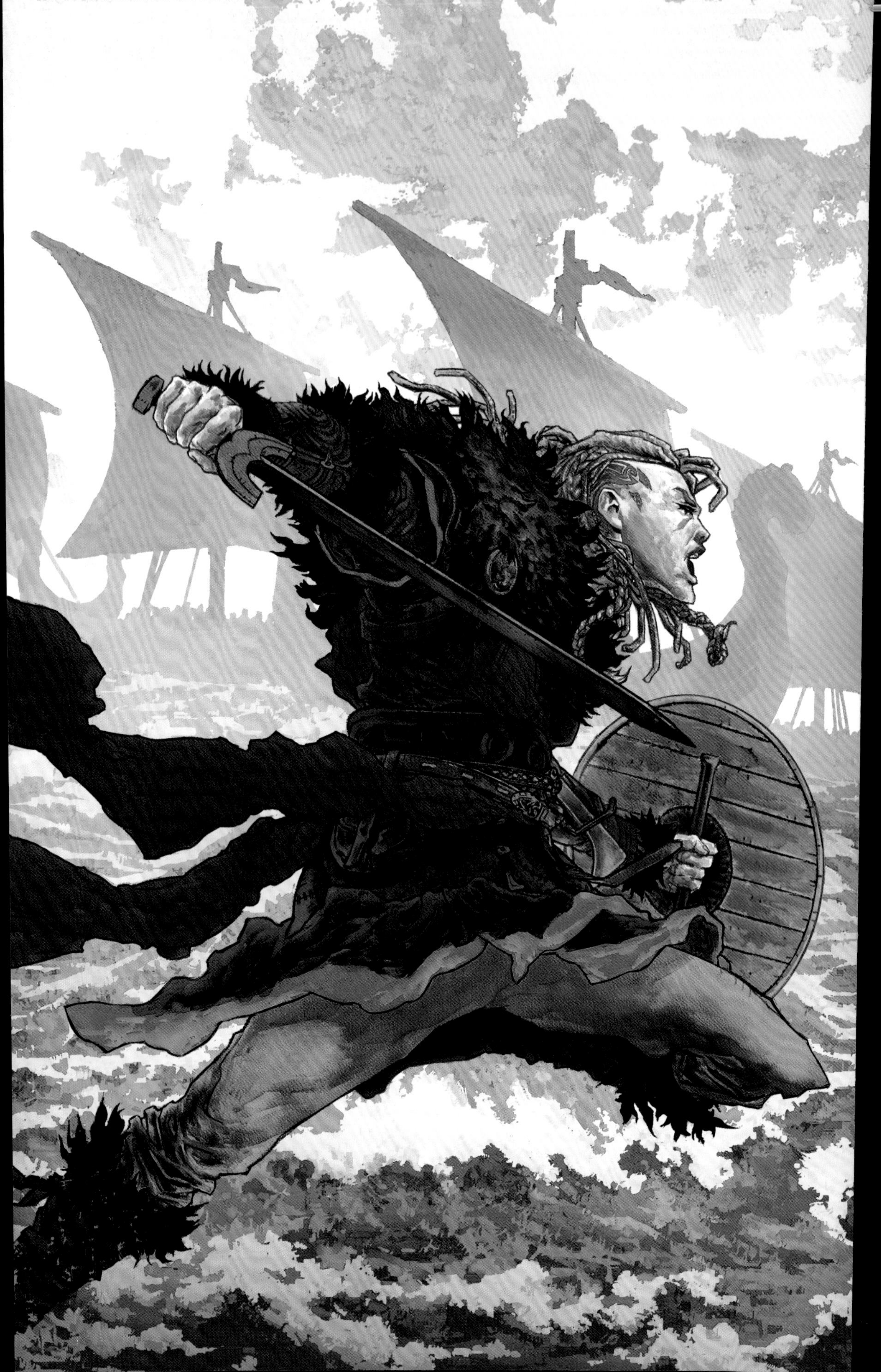

ASSASSIN'S CREED®

VALHALLA

SONG OF GLORY

CAVAN SCOTT // SCRIPT

MARTÍN TÚNICA // ART

MICHAEL ATIYEH // COLORS

**RICHARD STARKINGS AND COMICRAFT'S
JIMMY BETANCOURT** // LETTERS

KARL KOPINSKI // COVER ART

DARK HORSE BOOKS

MIKE RICHARDSON // PRESIDENT AND PUBLISHER

FREDDYE MILLER, DAVE MARSHALL // EDITORS

JUDY KHUU, KONNER KNUDSEN // ASSISTANT EDITORS

SARAH TERRY // DESIGNER

ALLYSON HALLER // DIGITAL ART TECHNICIAN

SPECIAL THANKS TO AYMAR AZAÏZIA, ANTOINE CESZYNSKI, FATIHA CHELLALI,
CAROLINE LAMACHE, ANTHONY MARCANTONIO, AND SUSAN PATRICK AT UBISOFT.

ASSASSIN'S CREED VALHALLA: SONG OF GLORY

This volume collects the Dark Horse comic book series *Assassin's Creed
Valhalla: Song of Glory* #1–#3, originally published October–December 2020.

Published by Dark Horse Books
A division of Dark Horse Comics LLC
10956 SE Main Street // Milwaukie, OR 97222

DarkHorse.com
To find a comics shop in your area, visit comicshoplocator.com

First edition: April 2021
Ebook ISBN 978-1-50671-930-6 // Hardcover ISBN 978-1-50671-929-0

10 9 8 7 6 5 4 3 2 1
Printed in China

Library of Congress Cataloging-in-Publication Data

Names: Scott, Cavan, author. | Túnica, Martín, artist. | Atiyeh, Michael,
   colourist. | Starkings, Richard, letterer. | Betancourt, Jimmy,
   letterer. | Kopinski, Karl, cover artist. | Ubisoft (Firm), sponsoring
   body.
Title: Assassin's Creed Valhalla : song of glory / script, Cavan Scott ;
   art, Martin Tunica ; colors, Michael Atiyeh ; letters, Richard Starkings
   and Comicraft's Jimmy Betancourt ; cover art, Karl Kopinski.
Other titles: Assassin's creed series (Video games)
Description: Milwaukie, OR : Dark Horse Books, 2021. | "Collects Assassin's
   Creed Valhalla: Song of Glory #1-#3"
Identifiers: LCCN 2020041455 | ISBN 9781506719290 (hardback) | ISBN
   9781506719306 (ebook)
Subjects: LCSH: Comic books, strips, etc.
Classification: LCC PN6738.A85 S36 2021 | DDC 741.5/942--dc23
LC record available at https://lccn.loc.gov/2020041455

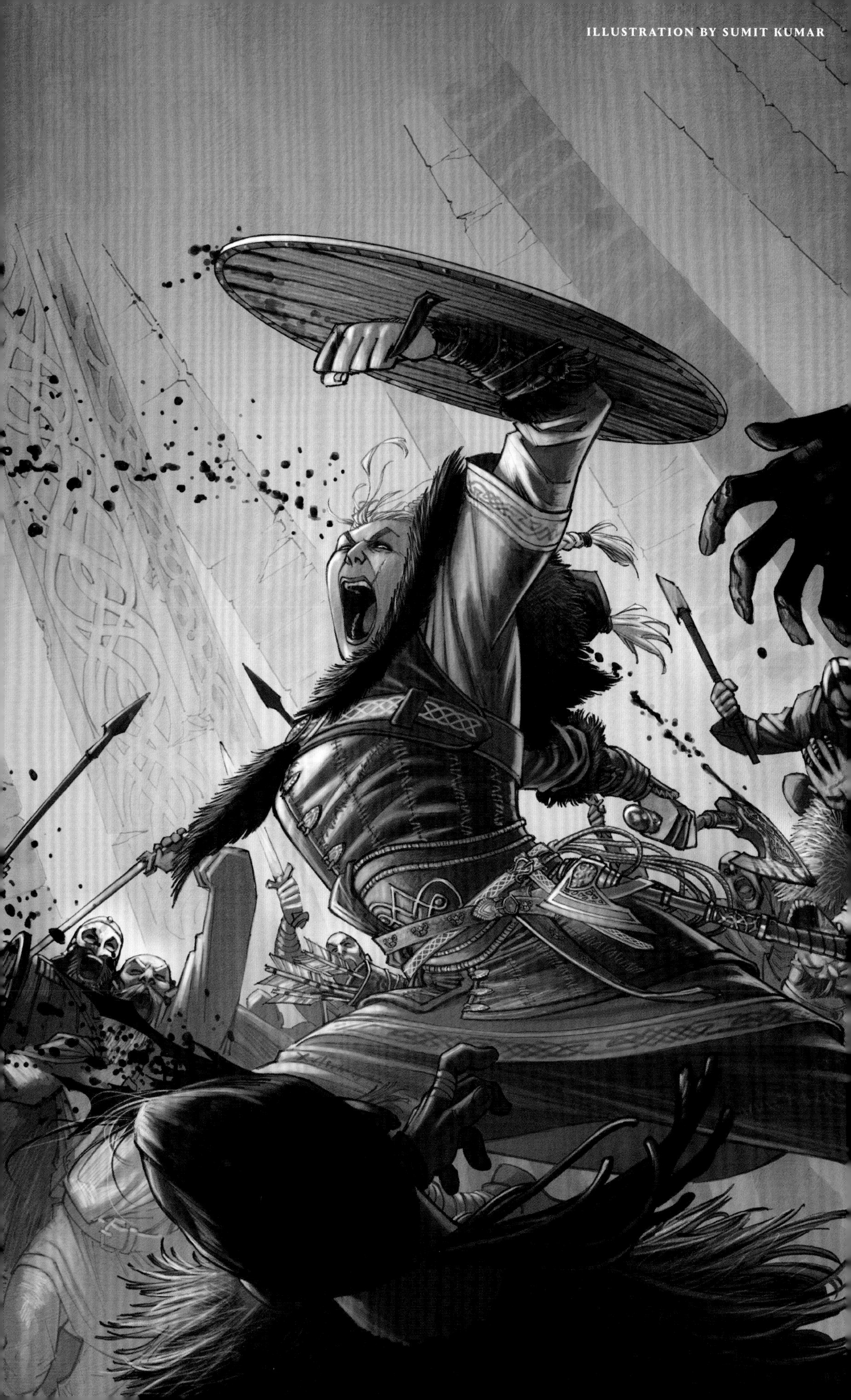

ILLUSTRATION BY SUMIT KUMAR

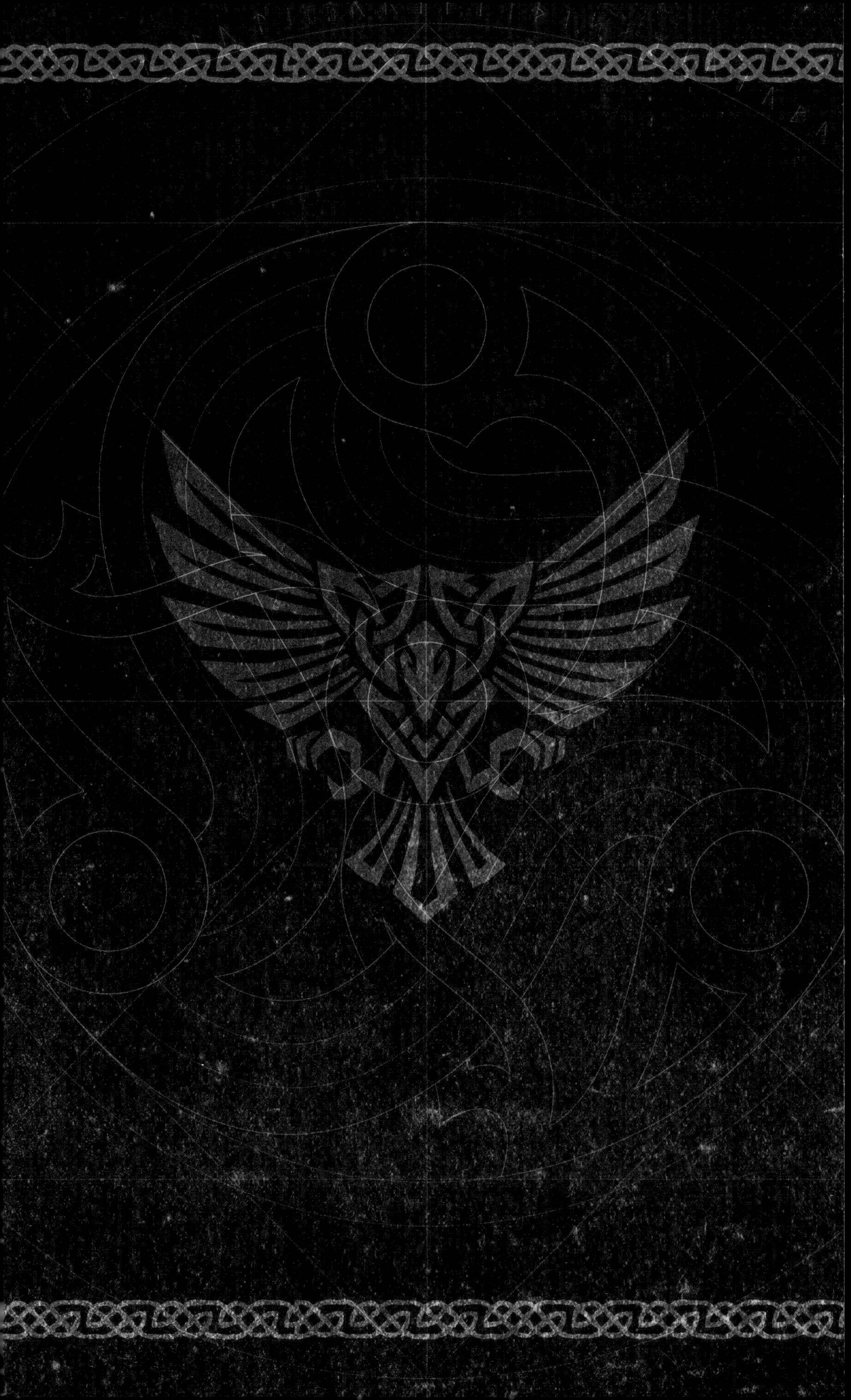

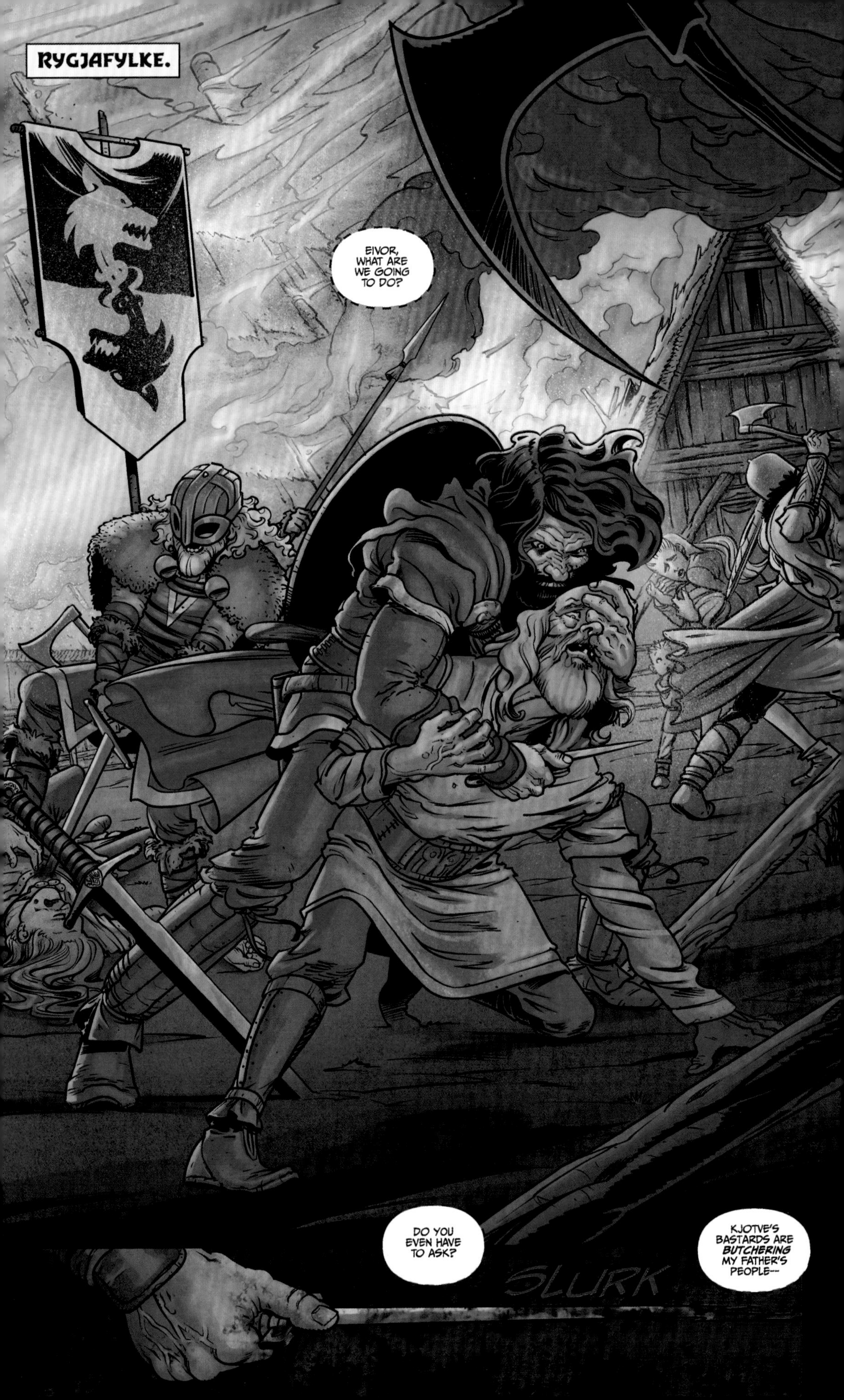
RYGJAFYLKE.
EIVOR, WHAT ARE WE GOING TO DO?
DO YOU EVEN HAVE TO ASK?
SLURK
KJOTVE'S BASTARDS ARE *BUTCHERING* MY FATHER'S PEOPLE---

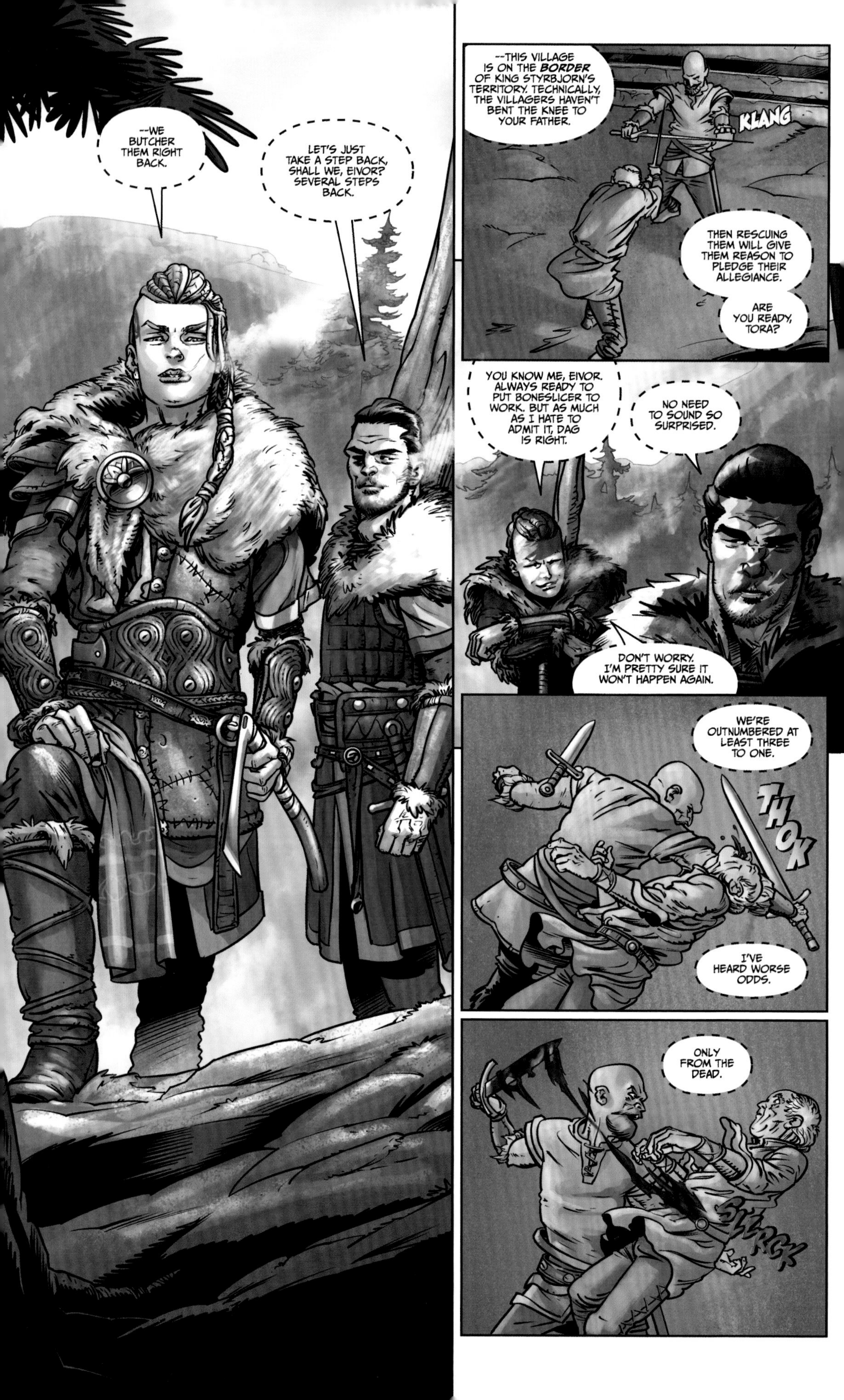
--WE BUTCHER THEM RIGHT BACK.
LET'S JUST TAKE A STEP BACK, SHALL WE, EIVOR? SEVERAL STEPS BACK.
--THIS VILLAGE IS ON THE BORDER OF KING STYRBJORN'S TERRITORY. TECHNICALLY, THE VILLAGERS HAVEN'T BENT THE KNEE TO YOUR FATHER.
KLANG
THEN RESCUING THEM WILL GIVE THEM REASON TO PLEDGE THEIR ALLEGIANCE.
ARE YOU READY, TORA?
YOU KNOW ME, EIVOR. ALWAYS READY TO PUT BONESLICER TO WORK. BUT AS MUCH AS I HATE TO ADMIT IT, DAG IS RIGHT.
NO NEED TO SOUND SO SURPRISED.
DON'T WORRY. I'M PRETTY SURE IT WON'T HAPPEN AGAIN.
WE'RE OUTNUMBERED AT LEAST THREE TO ONE.
THOK
I'VE HEARD WORSE ODDS.
ONLY FROM THE DEAD.
SHLRCK

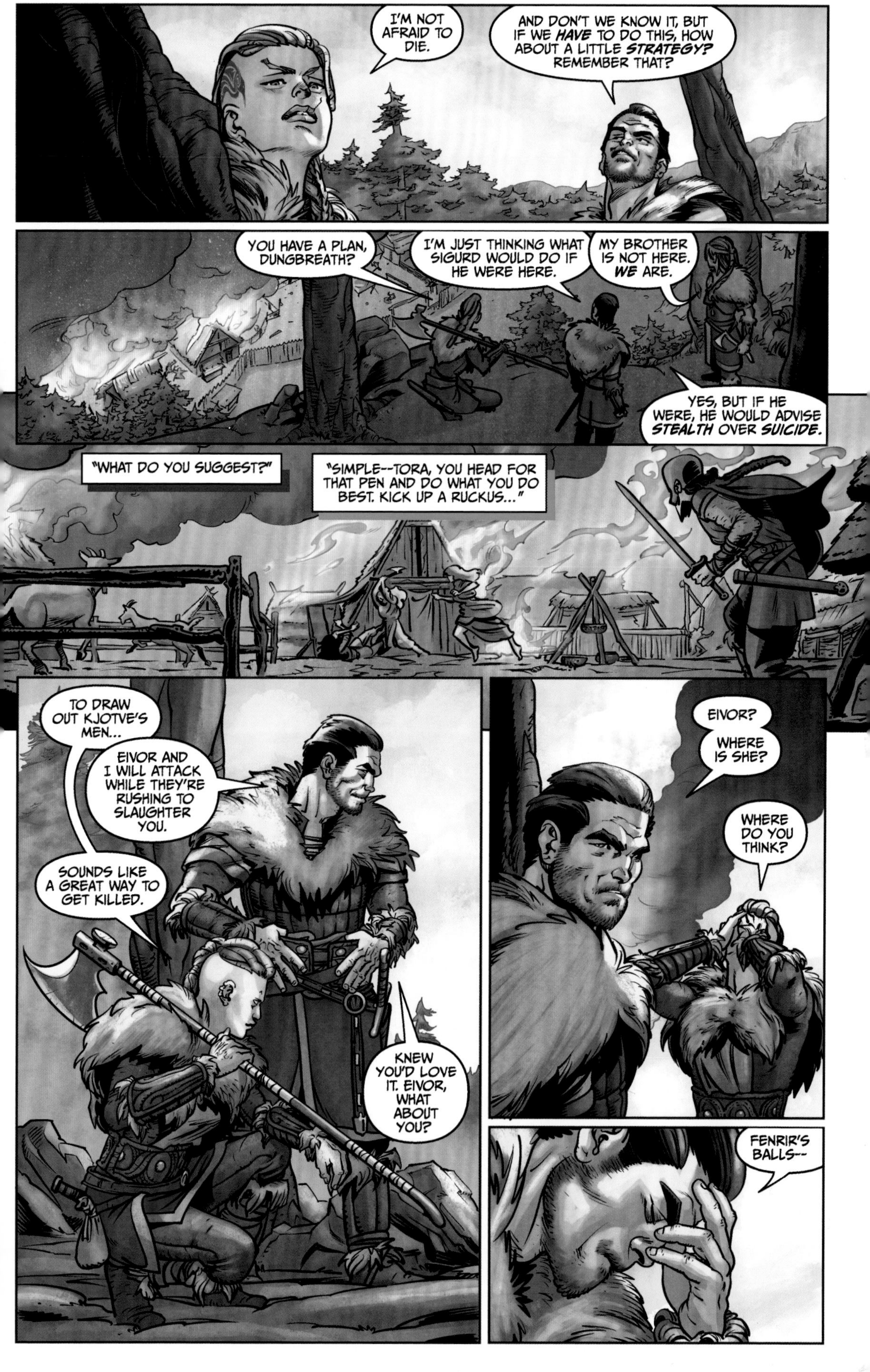
I'M NOT AFRAID TO DIE.
AND DON'T WE KNOW IT, BUT IF WE HAVE TO DO THIS, HOW ABOUT A LITTLE STRATEGY? REMEMBER THAT?
YOU HAVE A PLAN, DUNGBREATH?
I'M JUST THINKING WHAT SIGURD WOULD DO IF HE WERE HERE.
MY BROTHER IS NOT HERE. WE ARE.
YES, BUT IF HE WERE, HE WOULD ADVISE STEALTH OVER SUICIDE.
"WHAT DO YOU SUGGEST?"
"SIMPLE--TORA, YOU HEAD FOR THAT PEN AND DO WHAT YOU DO BEST. KICK UP A RUCKUS..."
TO DRAW OUT KJOTVE'S MEN...
EIVOR AND I WILL ATTACK WHILE THEY'RE RUSHING TO SLAUGHTER YOU.
SOUNDS LIKE A GREAT WAY TO GET KILLED.
KNEW YOU'D LOVE IT. EIVOR, WHAT ABOUT YOU?
EIVOR?
WHERE IS SHE?
WHERE DO YOU THINK?
FENRIR'S BALLS--

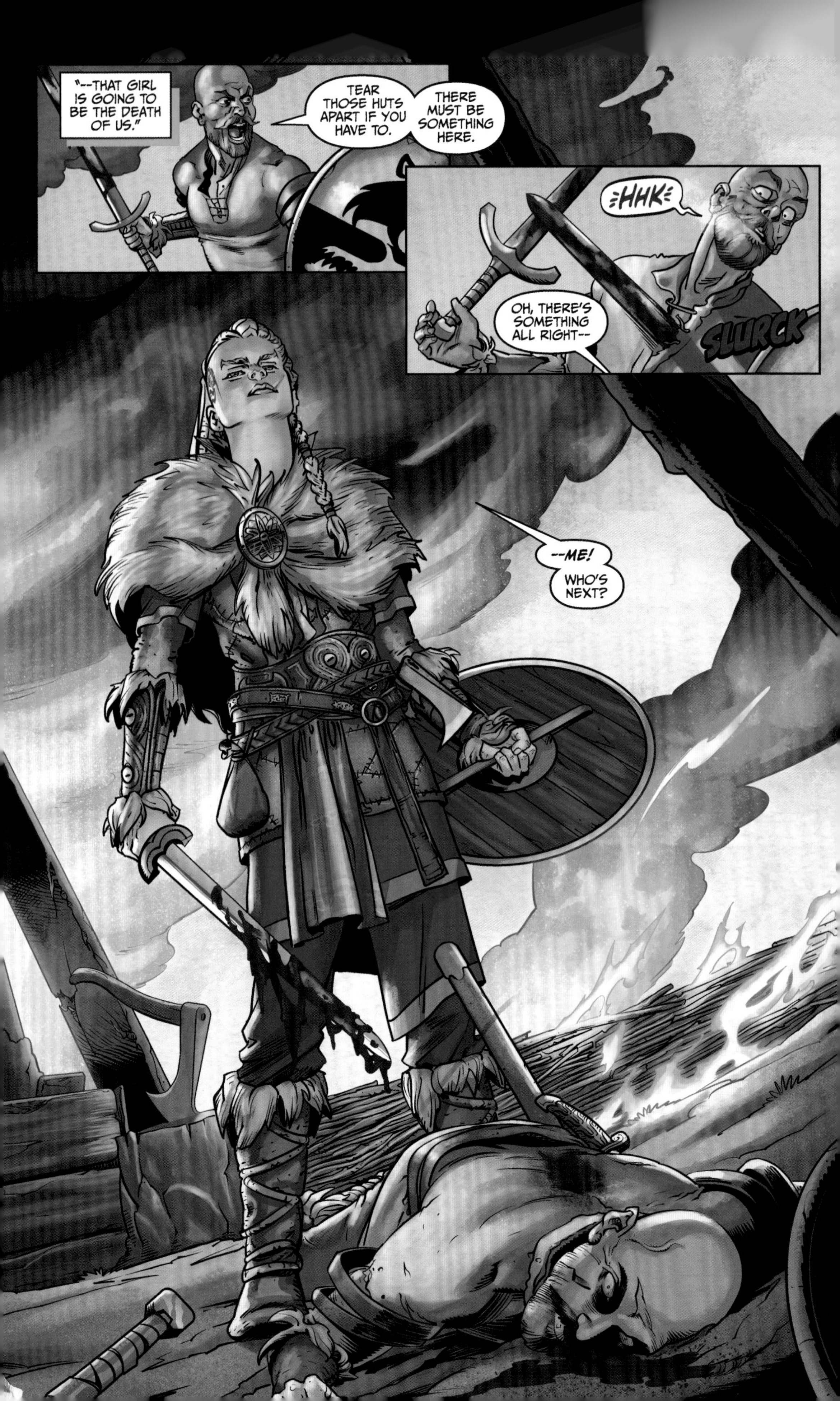

"--THAT GIRL IS GOING TO BE THE DEATH OF US."
TEAR THOSE HUTS APART IF YOU HAVE TO.
THERE MUST BE SOMETHING HERE.
HHK
OH, THERE'S SOMETHING ALL RIGHT--
SLURCK
--ME! WHO'S NEXT?

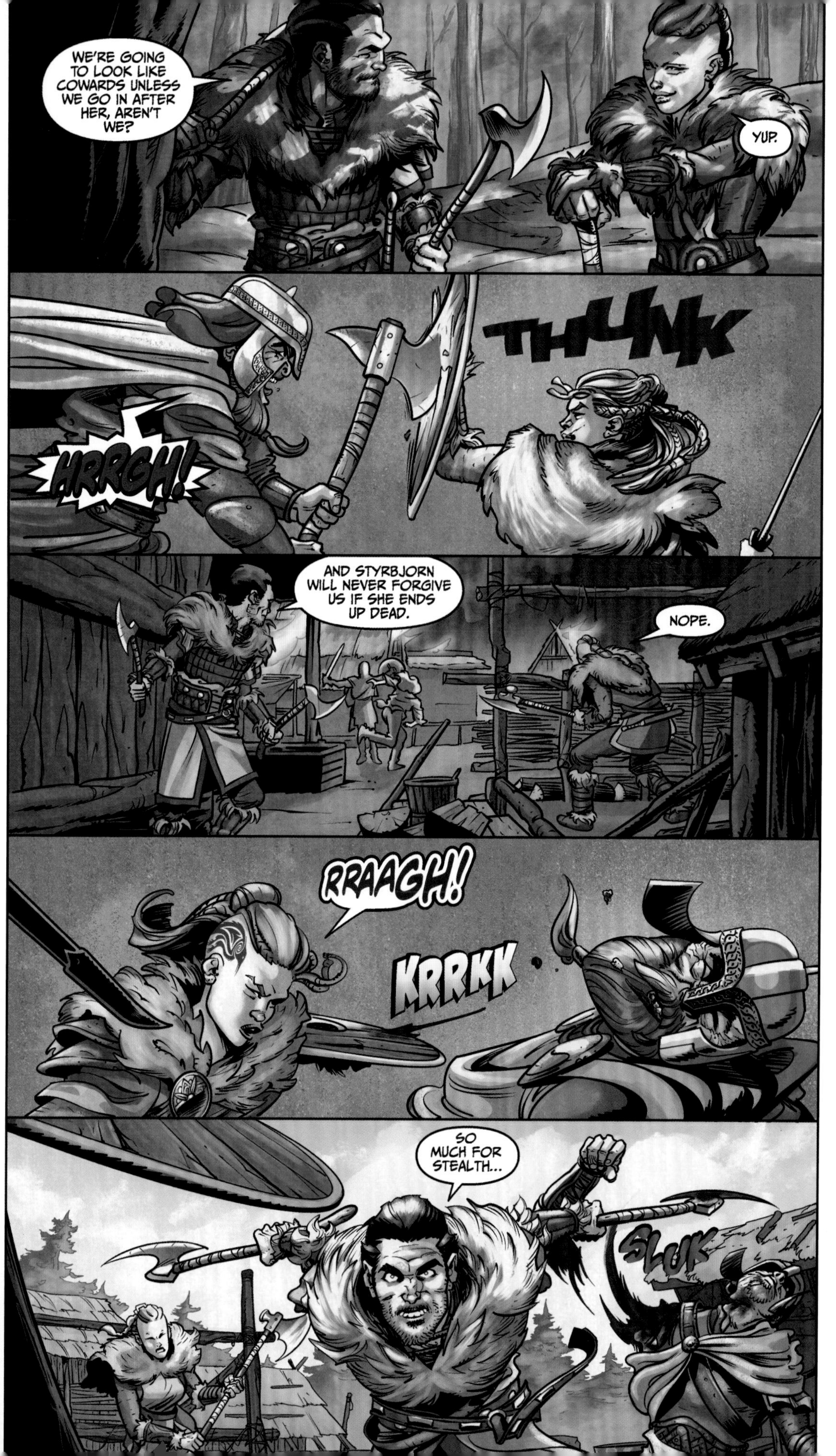
WE'RE GOING TO LOOK LIKE COWARDS UNLESS WE GO IN AFTER HER, AREN'T WE?
YUP.
THUNK
HRRGH!
AND STYRBJORN WILL NEVER FORGIVE US IF SHE ENDS UP DEAD.
NOPE.
RRAAGH!
KRRKK
SO MUCH FOR STEALTH...
SLUK

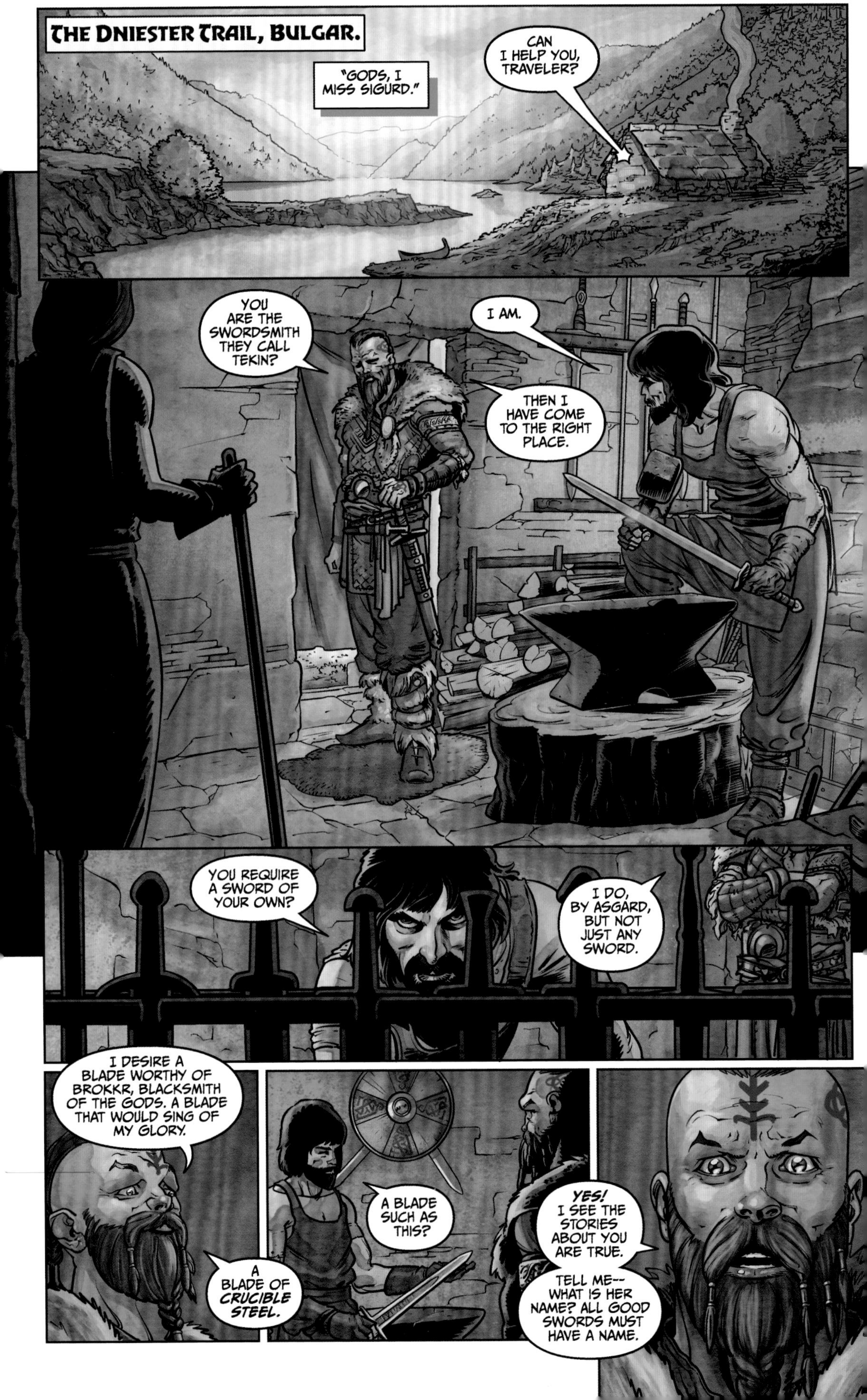
THE DNIESTER TRAIL, BULGAR.
"GODS, I MISS SIGURD."
CAN I HELP YOU, TRAVELER?
YOU ARE THE SWORDSMITH THEY CALL TEKIN?
I AM.
THEN I HAVE COME TO THE RIGHT PLACE.
YOU REQUIRE A SWORD OF YOUR OWN?
I DO, BY ASGARD, BUT NOT JUST ANY SWORD.
I DESIRE A BLADE WORTHY OF BROKKR, BLACKSMITH OF THE GODS. A BLADE THAT WOULD SING OF MY GLORY.
A BLADE OF CRUCIBLE STEEL.
A BLADE SUCH AS THIS?
YES! I SEE THE STORIES ABOUT YOU ARE TRUE.
TELL ME-- WHAT IS HER NAME? ALL GOOD SWORDS MUST HAVE A NAME.

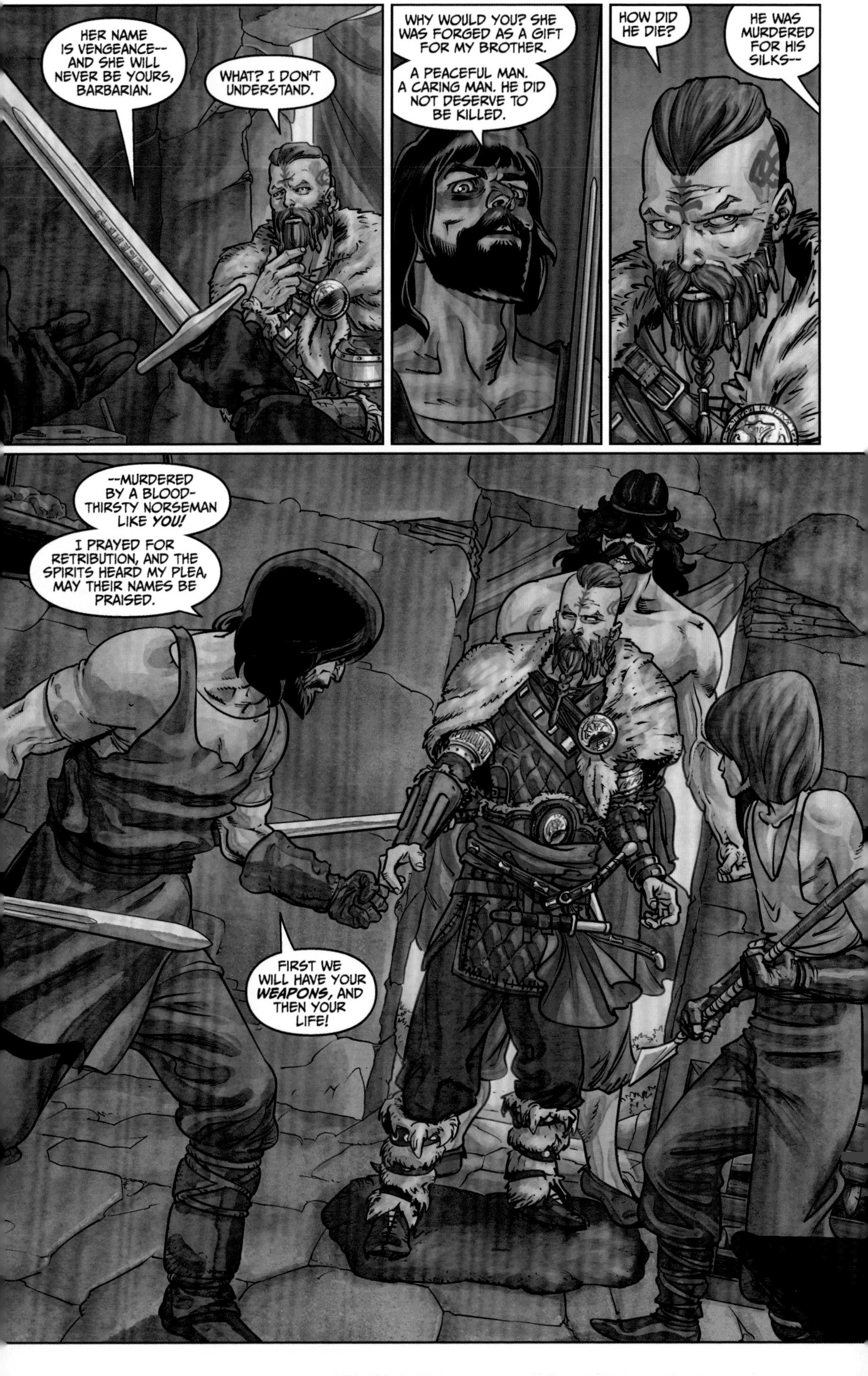

HER NAME IS VENGEANCE-- AND SHE WILL NEVER BE YOURS, BARBARIAN.
WHAT? I DON'T UNDERSTAND.
WHY WOULD YOU? SHE WAS FORGED AS A GIFT FOR MY BROTHER.
A PEACEFUL MAN. A CARING MAN. HE DID NOT DESERVE TO BE KILLED.
HOW DID HE DIE?
HE WAS MURDERED FOR HIS SILKS--
--MURDERED BY A BLOOD-THIRSTY NORSEMAN LIKE *YOU!*
I PRAYED FOR RETRIBUTION, AND THE SPIRITS HEARD MY PLEA, MAY THEIR NAMES BE PRAISED.
FIRST WE WILL HAVE YOUR ***WEAPONS,*** AND THEN YOUR LIFE!

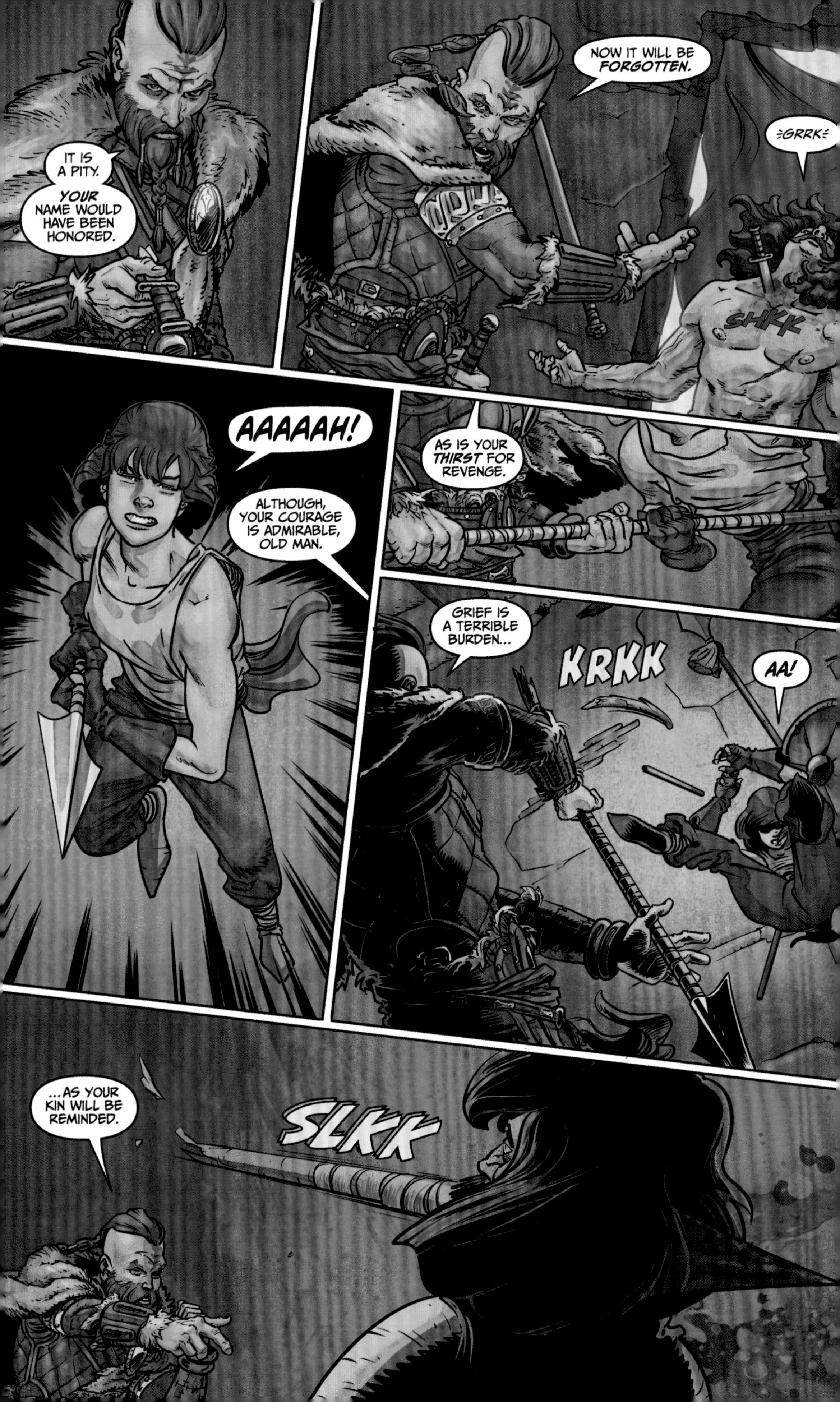
IT IS A PITY. YOUR NAME WOULD HAVE BEEN HONORED.
NOW IT WILL BE FORGOTTEN.
GRRK
SHKK
AAAAAH!
ALTHOUGH, YOUR COURAGE IS ADMIRABLE, OLD MAN.
AS IS YOUR THIRST FOR REVENGE.
GRIEF IS A TERRIBLE BURDEN...
KRKK
AA!
...AS YOUR KIN WILL BE REMINDED.
SLKK

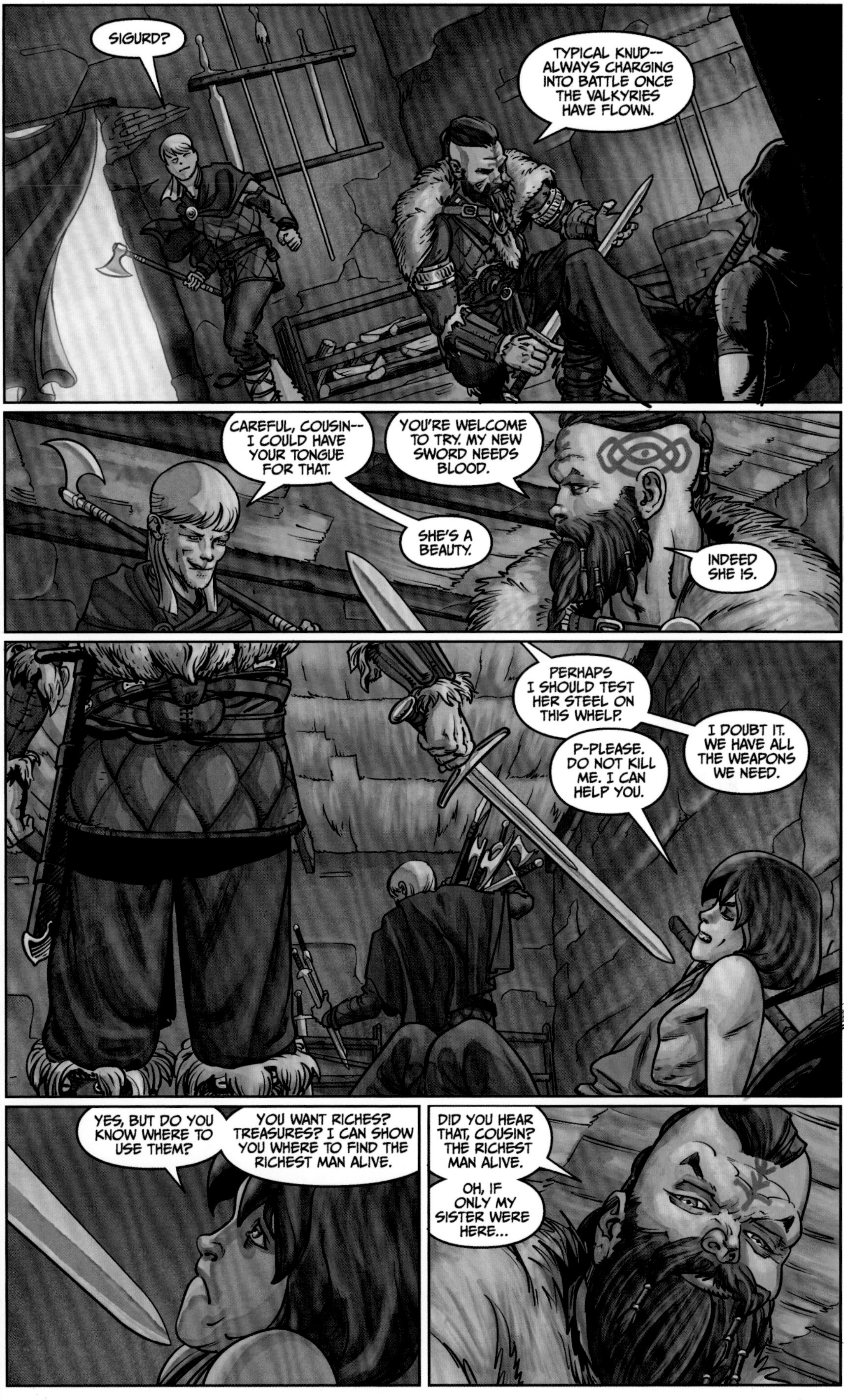

SIGURD?
TYPICAL KNUD-- ALWAYS CHARGING INTO BATTLE ONCE THE VALKYRIES HAVE FLOWN.
CAREFUL, COUSIN-- I COULD HAVE YOUR TONGUE FOR THAT.
YOU'RE WELCOME TO TRY. MY NEW SWORD NEEDS BLOOD.
SHE'S A BEAUTY.
INDEED SHE IS.
PERHAPS I SHOULD TEST HER STEEL ON THIS WHELP.
P-PLEASE. DO NOT KILL ME. I CAN HELP YOU.
I DOUBT IT. WE HAVE ALL THE WEAPONS WE NEED.
YES, BUT DO YOU KNOW WHERE TO USE THEM?
YOU WANT RICHES? TREASURES? I CAN SHOW YOU WHERE TO FIND THE RICHEST MAN ALIVE.
DID YOU HEAR THAT, COUSIN? THE RICHEST MAN ALIVE.
OH, IF ONLY MY SISTER WERE HERE...

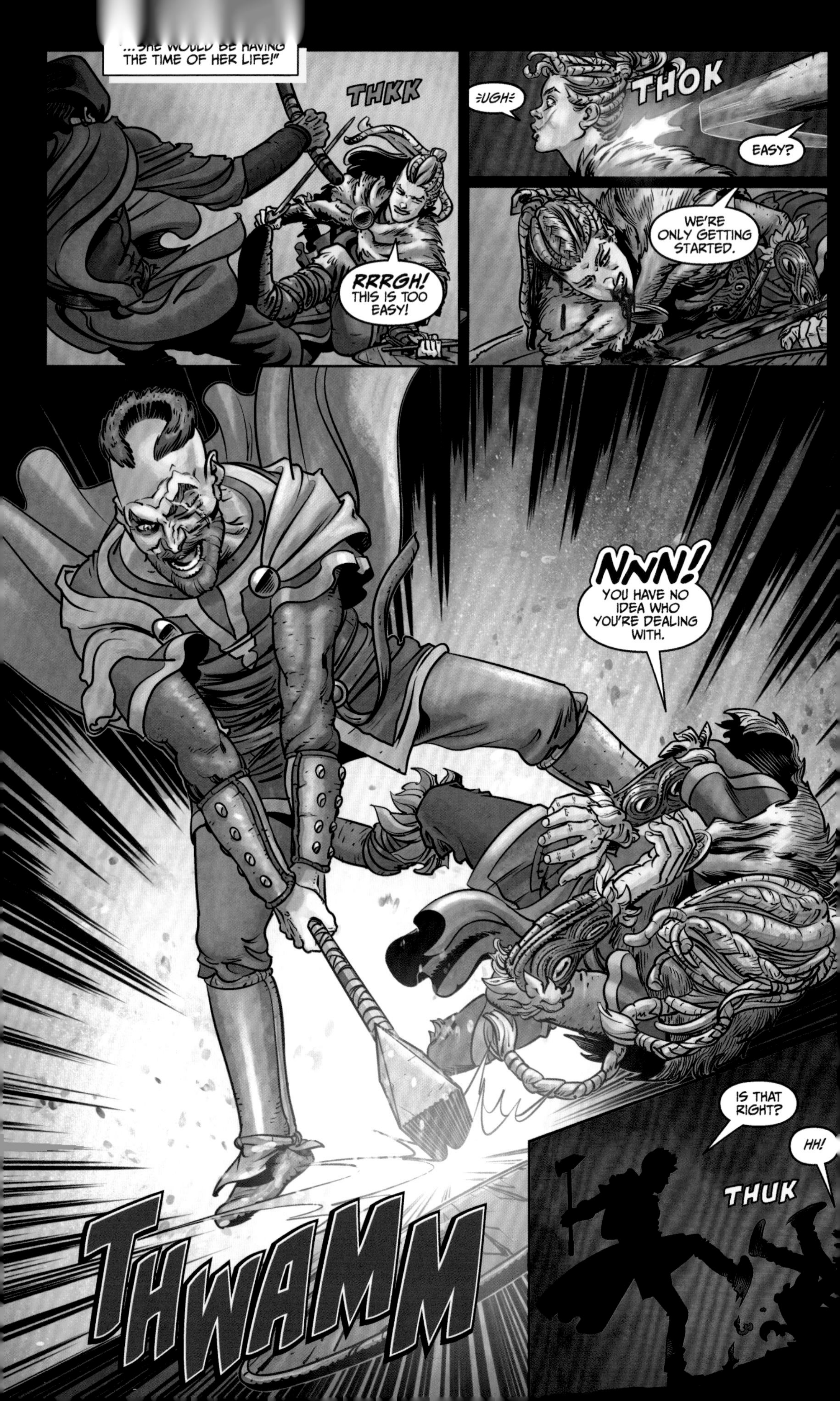
"...SHE WOULD BE HAVING THE TIME OF HER LIFE!"
THKK
RRRGH! THIS IS TOO EASY!
UGH
THOK
EASY?
WE'RE ONLY GETTING STARTED.
NNN! YOU HAVE NO IDEA WHO YOU'RE DEALING WITH.
THWAMM
IS THAT RIGHT?
HH!
THUK

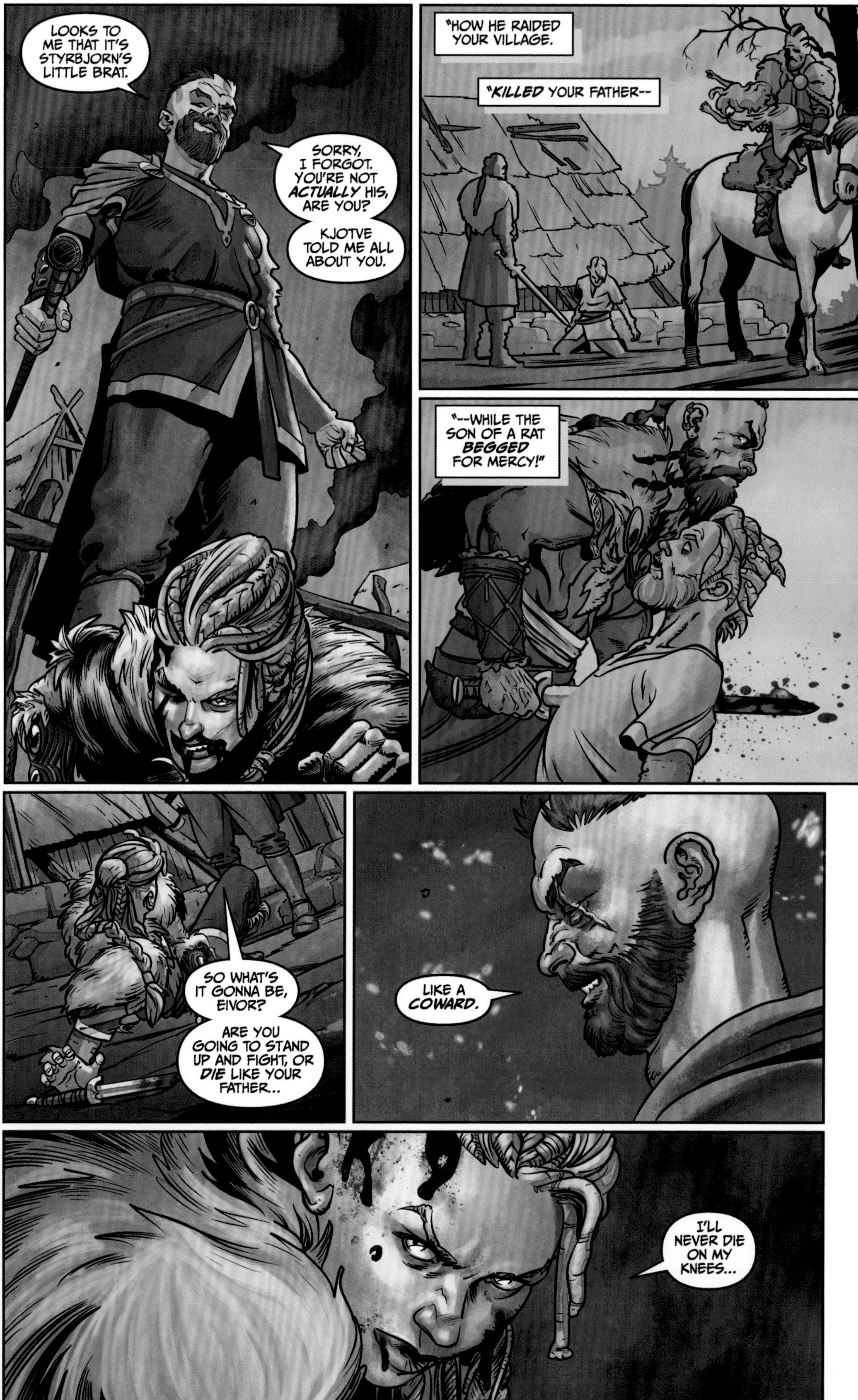
LOOKS TO ME THAT IT'S STYRBJORN'S LITTLE BRAT.
SORRY, I FORGOT. YOU'RE NOT ACTUALLY HIS, ARE YOU?
KJOTVE TOLD ME ALL ABOUT YOU.
"HOW HE RAIDED YOUR VILLAGE.
"KILLED YOUR FATHER--
"--WHILE THE SON OF A RAT BEGGED FOR MERCY!"
SO WHAT'S IT GONNA BE, EIVOR?
ARE YOU GOING TO STAND UP AND FIGHT, OR DIE LIKE YOUR FATHER...
LIKE A COWARD.
I'LL NEVER DIE ON MY KNEES...

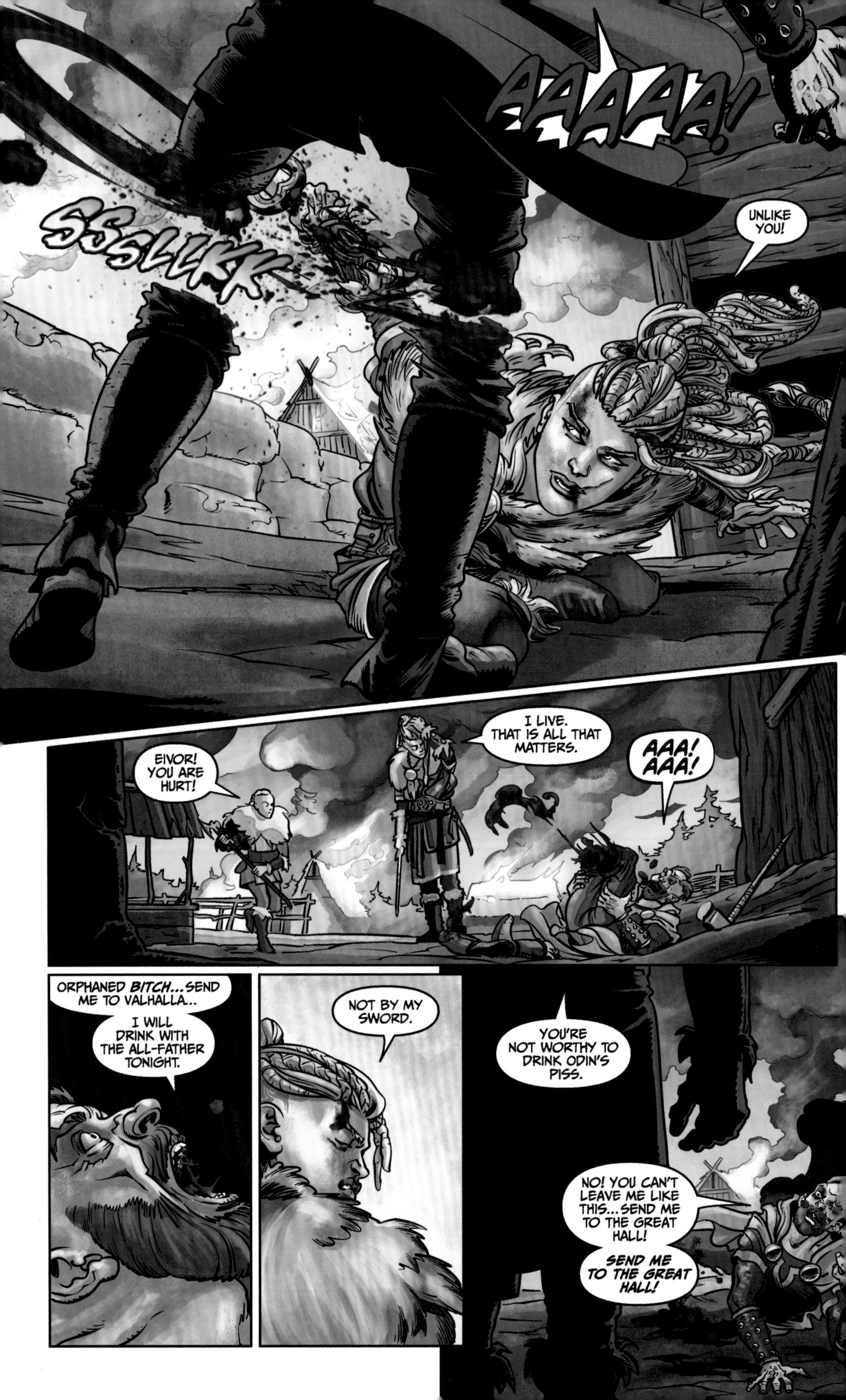
AAAAAA!
SSSLIKK
UNLIKE YOU!
EIVOR! YOU ARE HURT!
I LIVE. THAT IS ALL THAT MATTERS.
AAA! AAA!
ORPHANED *BITCH*...SEND ME TO VALHALLA...
I WILL DRINK WITH THE ALL-FATHER TONIGHT.
NOT BY MY SWORD.
YOU'RE NOT WORTHY TO DRINK ODIN'S PISS.
NO! YOU CAN'T LEAVE ME LIKE THIS...SEND ME TO THE GREAT HALL!
SEND ME TO THE GREAT HALL!

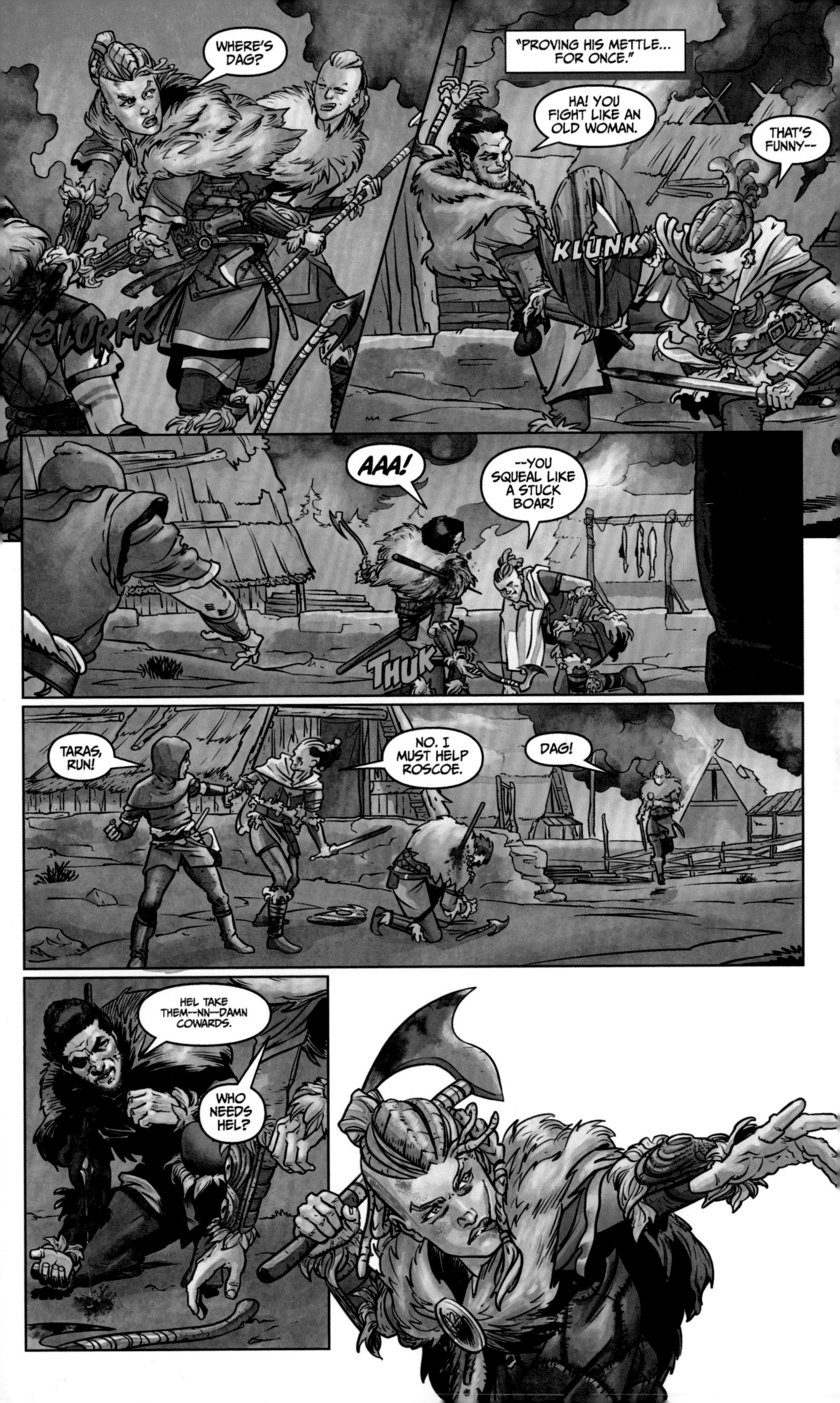
WHERE'S DAG?
"PROVING HIS METTLE... FOR ONCE."
SLURKK
HA! YOU FIGHT LIKE AN OLD WOMAN.
THAT'S FUNNY--
KLUNK
AAA!
--YOU SQUEAL LIKE A STUCK BOAR!
THUK
TARAS, RUN!
NO. I MUST HELP ROSCOE.
DAG!
HEL TAKE THEM--NN--DAMN COWARDS.
WHO NEEDS HEL?

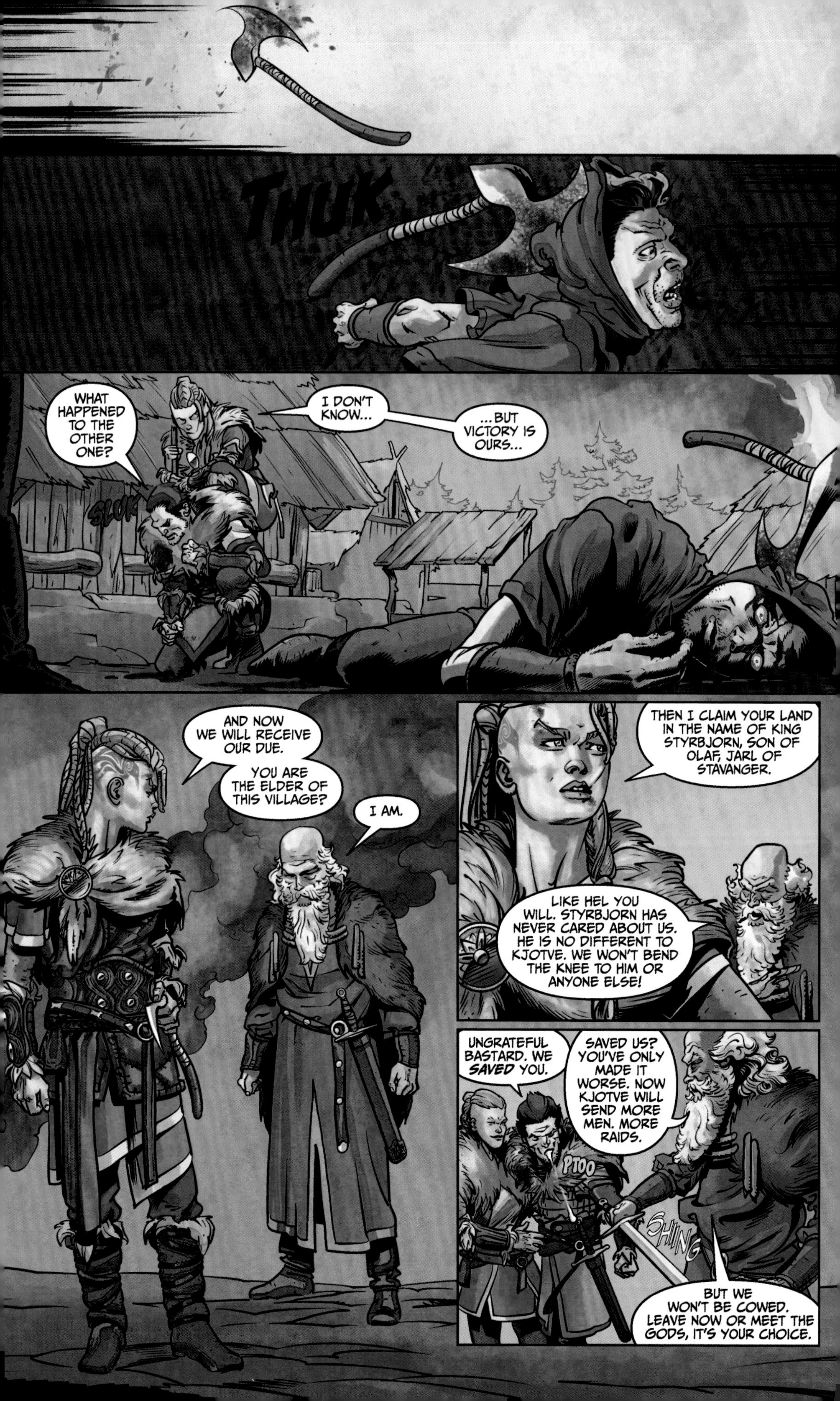
THUK
WHAT HAPPENED TO THE OTHER ONE?
I DON'T KNOW...
...BUT VICTORY IS OURS...
SLOK
AND NOW WE WILL RECEIVE OUR DUE.
YOU ARE THE ELDER OF THIS VILLAGE?
I AM.
THEN I CLAIM YOUR LAND IN THE NAME OF KING STYRBJORN, SON OF OLAF, JARL OF STAVANGER.
LIKE HEL YOU WILL. STYRBJORN HAS NEVER CARED ABOUT US. HE IS NO DIFFERENT TO KJOTVE. WE WON'T BEND THE KNEE TO HIM OR ANYONE ELSE!
UNGRATEFUL BASTARD. WE *SAVED* YOU.
SAVED US? YOU'VE ONLY MADE IT WORSE. NOW KJOTVE WILL SEND MORE MEN. MORE RAIDS.
PTOO
SHING
BUT WE WON'T BE COWED. LEAVE NOW OR MEET THE GODS, IT'S YOUR CHOICE.

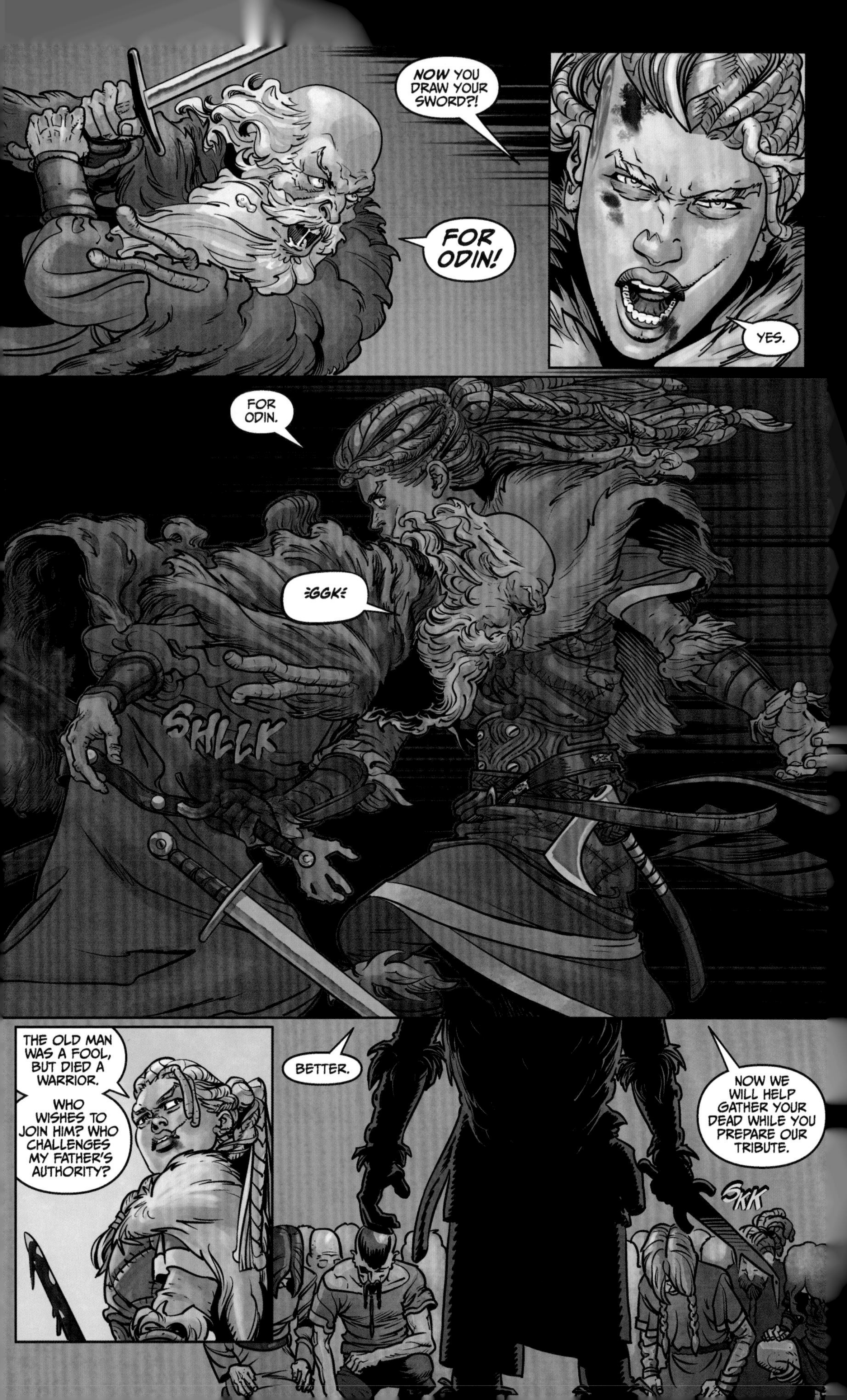
NOW YOU DRAW YOUR SWORD?!
FOR ODIN!
YES.
FOR ODIN.
GGK
SHLLK
THE OLD MAN WAS A FOOL, BUT DIED A WARRIOR.
WHO WISHES TO JOIN HIM? WHO CHALLENGES MY FATHER'S AUTHORITY?
BETTER.
NOW WE WILL HELP GATHER YOUR DEAD WHILE YOU PREPARE OUR TRIBUTE.
SKK

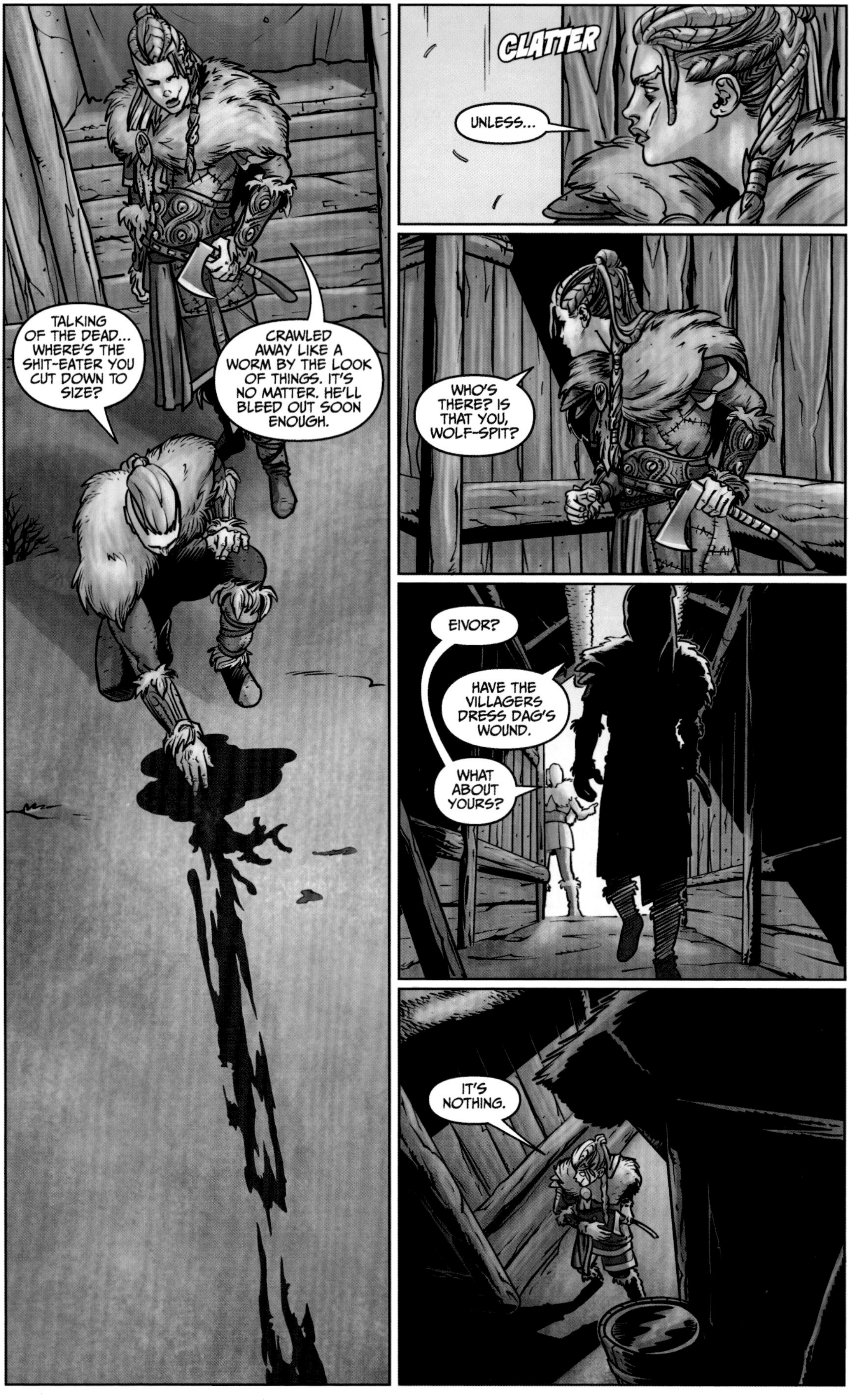
TALKING OF THE DEAD... WHERE'S THE SHIT-EATER YOU CUT DOWN TO SIZE?
CRAWLED AWAY LIKE A WORM BY THE LOOK OF THINGS. IT'S NO MATTER. HE'LL BLEED OUT SOON ENOUGH.
CLATTER
UNLESS...
WHO'S THERE? IS THAT YOU, WOLF-SPIT?
EIVOR?
HAVE THE VILLAGERS DRESS DAG'S WOUND.
WHAT ABOUT YOURS?
IT'S NOTHING.

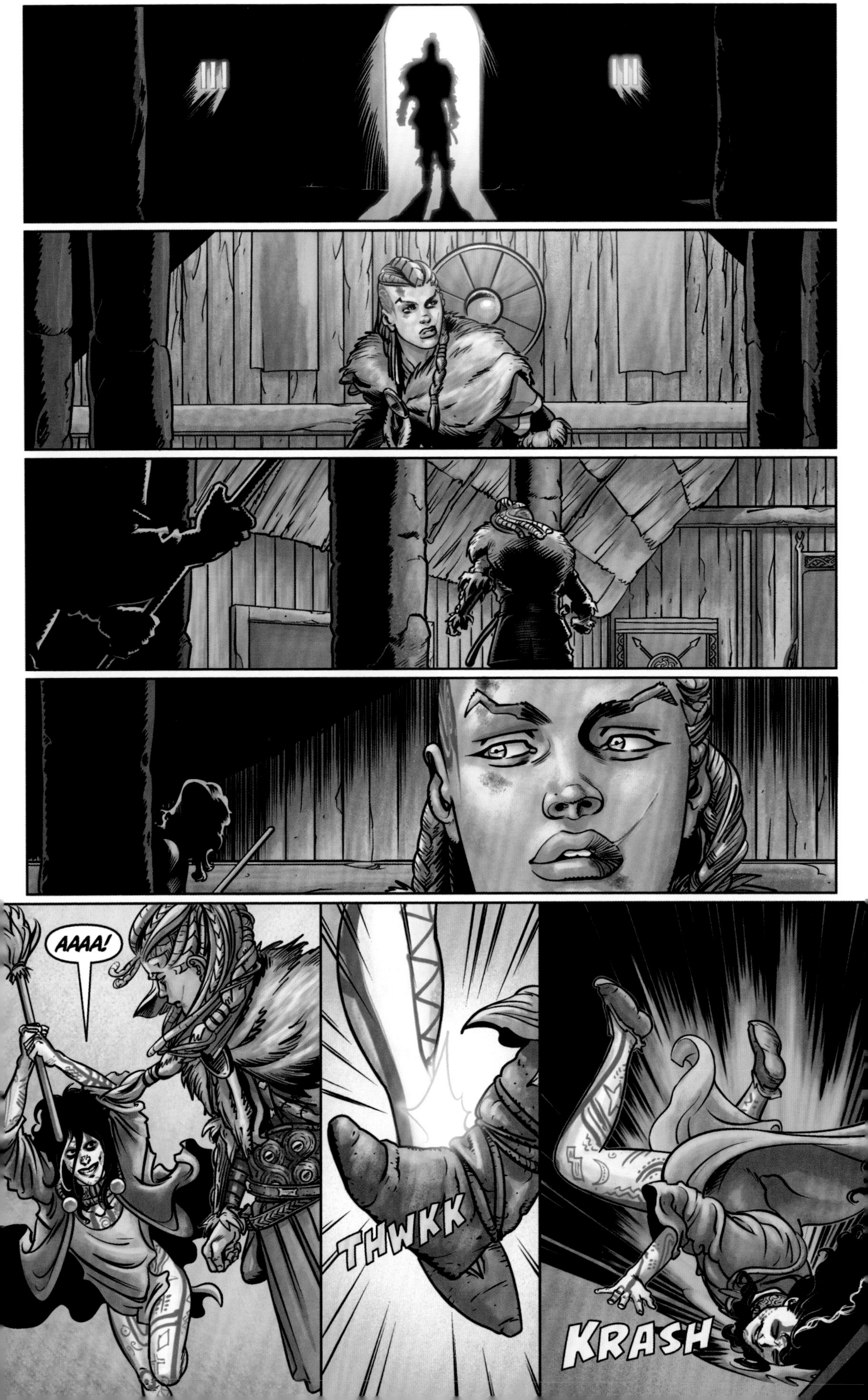
AAAA!
THWKK
KRASH

YOU'RE A SLAVE.

YES. GULL IS A SLAVE. SLAVE TO KJOTVE. SLAVE TO THE NORNS. SLAVE TO SÖKKVABEKKR, SÁGA AND IDUN'S BOUNTY.

BUT WHO ARE YOU?

WHAT FACE DO YOU WEAR?

WHOSE SOUL DO YOU HIDE?

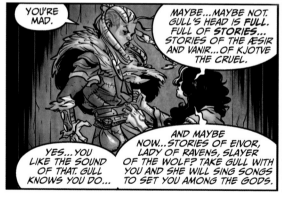

YOU'RE MAD.

MAYBE...MAYBE NOT. GULL'S HEAD IS FULL. FULL OF STORIES... STORIES OF THE ÆSIR AND VANIR...OF KJOTVE THE CRUEL.

YES...YOU LIKE THE SOUND OF THAT. GULL KNOWS YOU DO...

AND MAYBE NOW...STORIES OF EIVOR, LADY OF RAVENS, SLAYER OF THE WOLF? TAKE GULL WITH YOU AND SHE WILL SING SONGS TO SET YOU AMONG THE GODS.

GULL IS WISER THAN SHE LOOKS. YES. YOU WILL MAKE A FINE GIFT.

A GIFT? FOR WHO? THE HANGED GOD HIMSELF?

NO... BUT THE NEXT BEST THING...

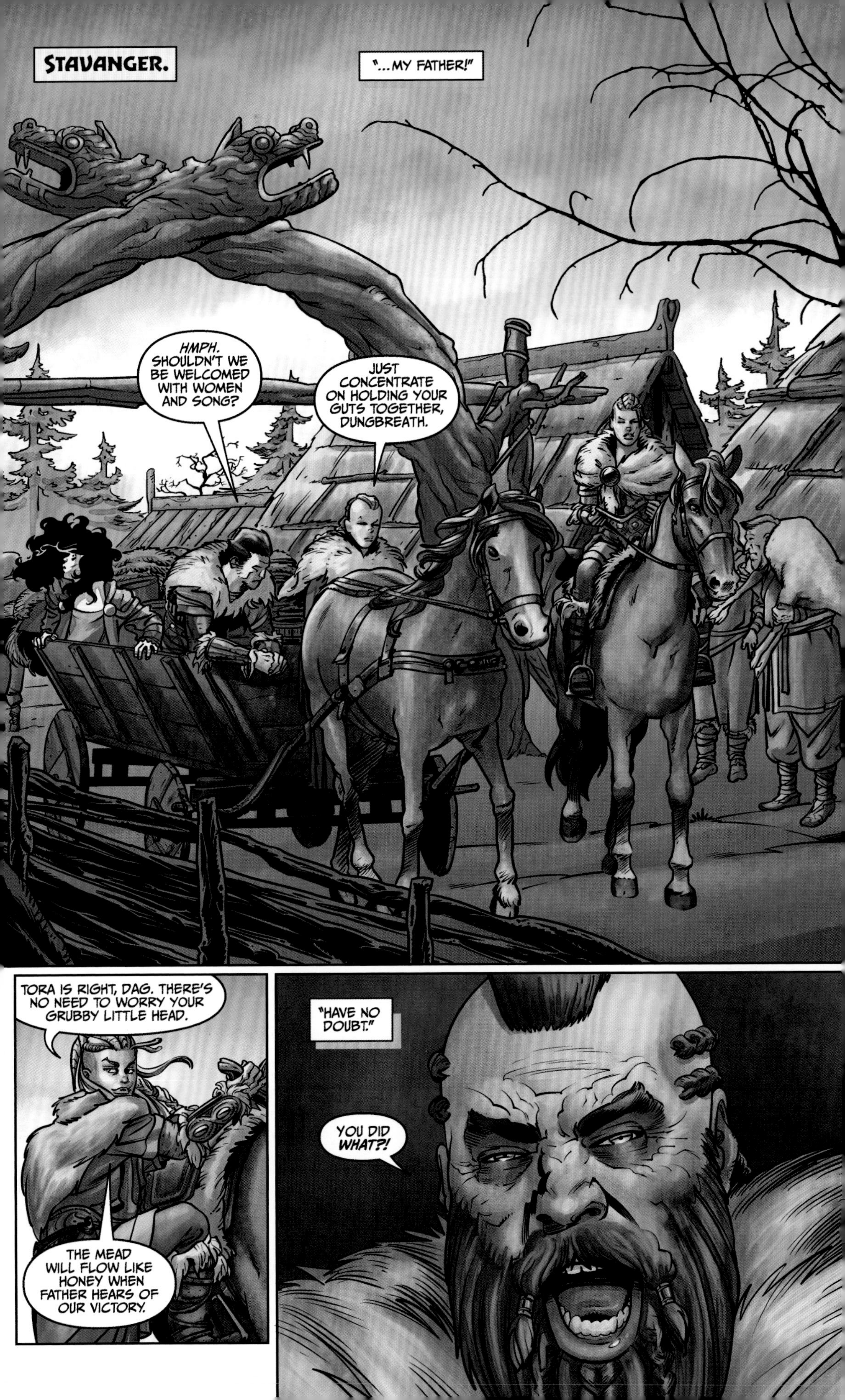
STAVANGER.
"...MY FATHER!"
HMPH. SHOULDN'T WE BE WELCOMED WITH WOMEN AND SONG?
JUST CONCENTRATE ON HOLDING YOUR GUTS TOGETHER, DUNGBREATH.
TORA IS RIGHT, DAG. THERE'S NO NEED TO WORRY YOUR GRUBBY LITTLE HEAD.
THE MEAD WILL FLOW LIKE HONEY WHEN FATHER HEARS OF OUR VICTORY.
"HAVE NO DOUBT."
YOU DID WHAT?!

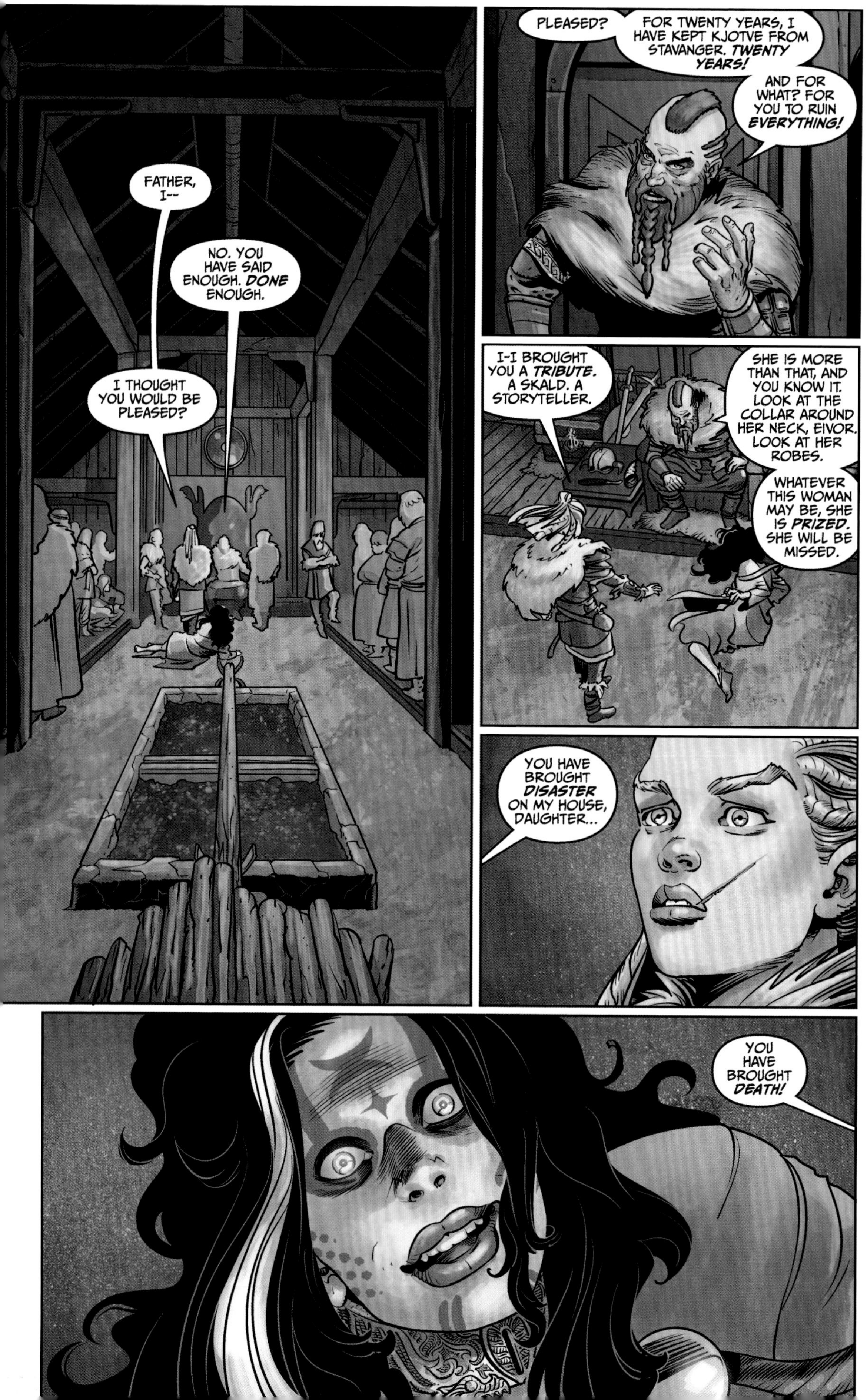
FATHER, I--
NO. YOU HAVE SAID ENOUGH. DONE ENOUGH.
I THOUGHT YOU WOULD BE PLEASED?
PLEASED?
FOR TWENTY YEARS, I HAVE KEPT KJOTVE FROM STAVANGER. TWENTY YEARS!
AND FOR WHAT? FOR YOU TO RUIN EVERYTHING!
I-I BROUGHT YOU A TRIBUTE. A SKALD. A STORYTELLER.
SHE IS MORE THAN THAT, AND YOU KNOW IT. LOOK AT THE COLLAR AROUND HER NECK, EIVOR. LOOK AT HER ROBES.
WHATEVER THIS WOMAN MAY BE, SHE IS PRIZED. SHE WILL BE MISSED.
YOU HAVE BROUGHT DISASTER ON MY HOUSE, DAUGHTER...
YOU HAVE BROUGHT DEATH!

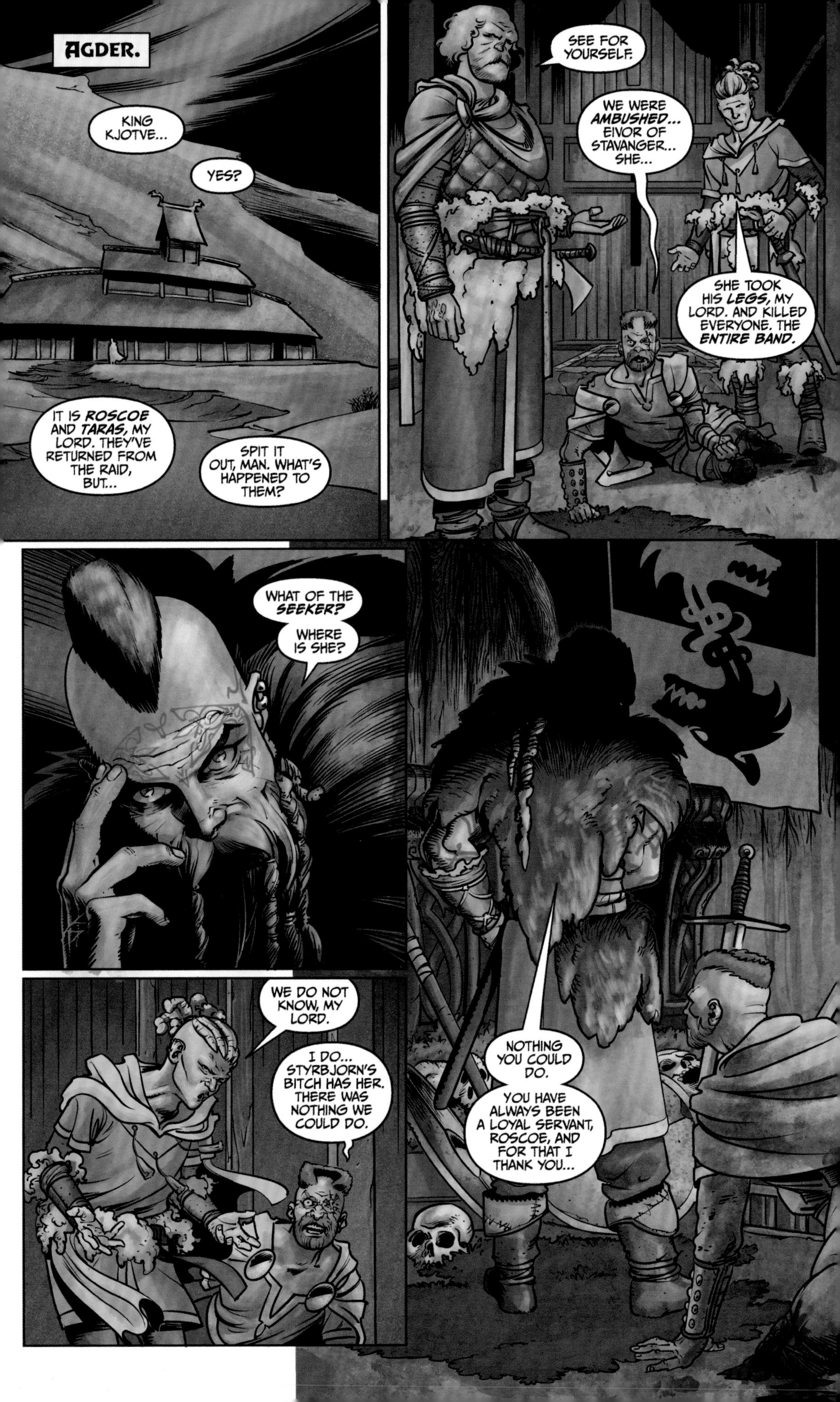
AGDER.
KING KJOTVE...
YES?
IT IS ROSCOE AND TARAS, MY LORD. THEY'VE RETURNED FROM THE RAID, BUT...
SPIT IT OUT, MAN. WHAT'S HAPPENED TO THEM?
SEE FOR YOURSELF.
WE WERE AMBUSHED... EIVOR OF STAVANGER... SHE...
SHE TOOK HIS LEGS, MY LORD. AND KILLED EVERYONE. THE ENTIRE BAND.
WHAT OF THE SEEKER?
WHERE IS SHE?
WE DO NOT KNOW, MY LORD.
I DO... STYRBJORN'S BITCH HAS HER. THERE WAS NOTHING WE COULD DO.
NOTHING YOU COULD DO.
YOU HAVE ALWAYS BEEN A LOYAL SERVANT, ROSCOE, AND FOR THAT I THANK YOU...

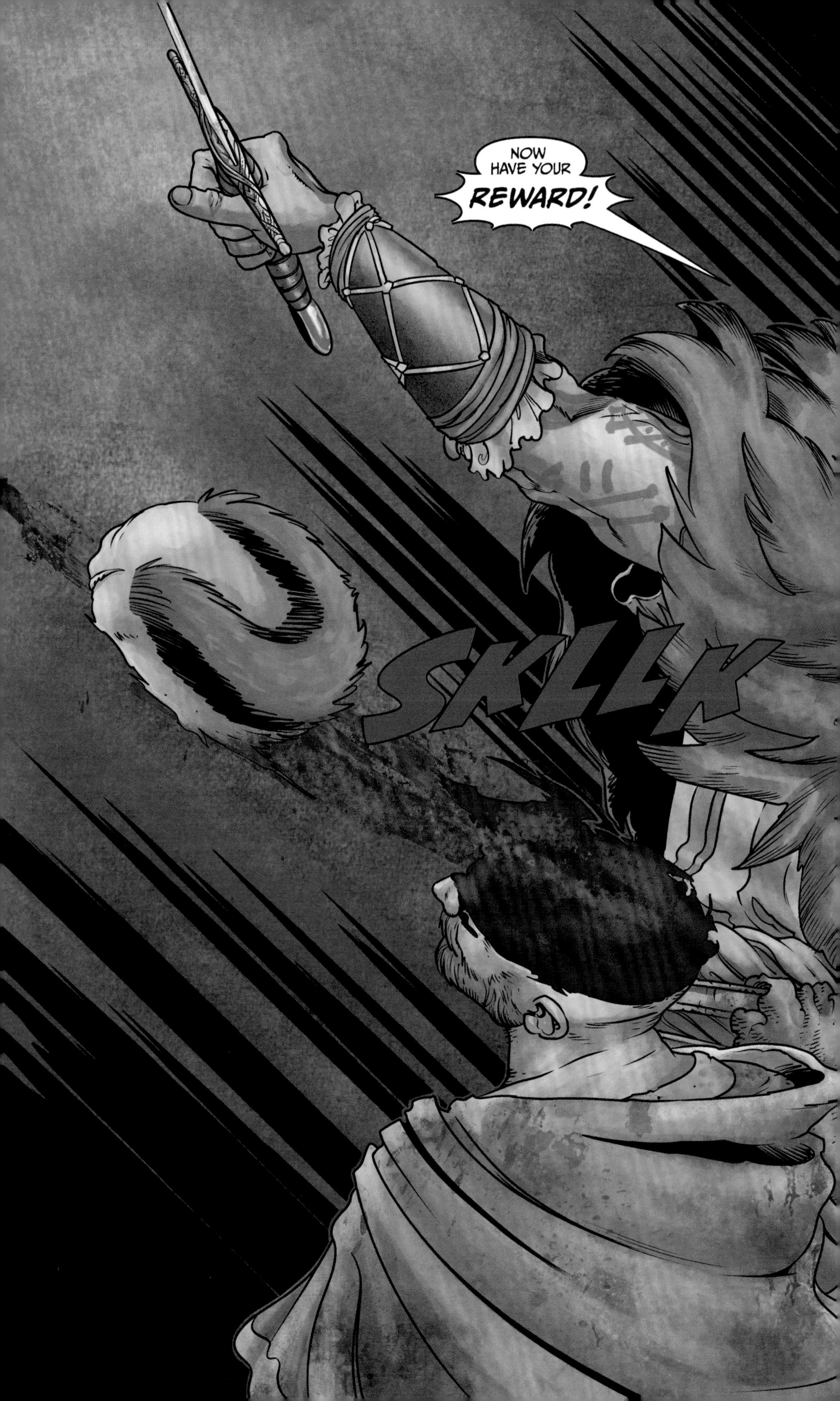
NOW HAVE YOUR REWARD!
SKLLK

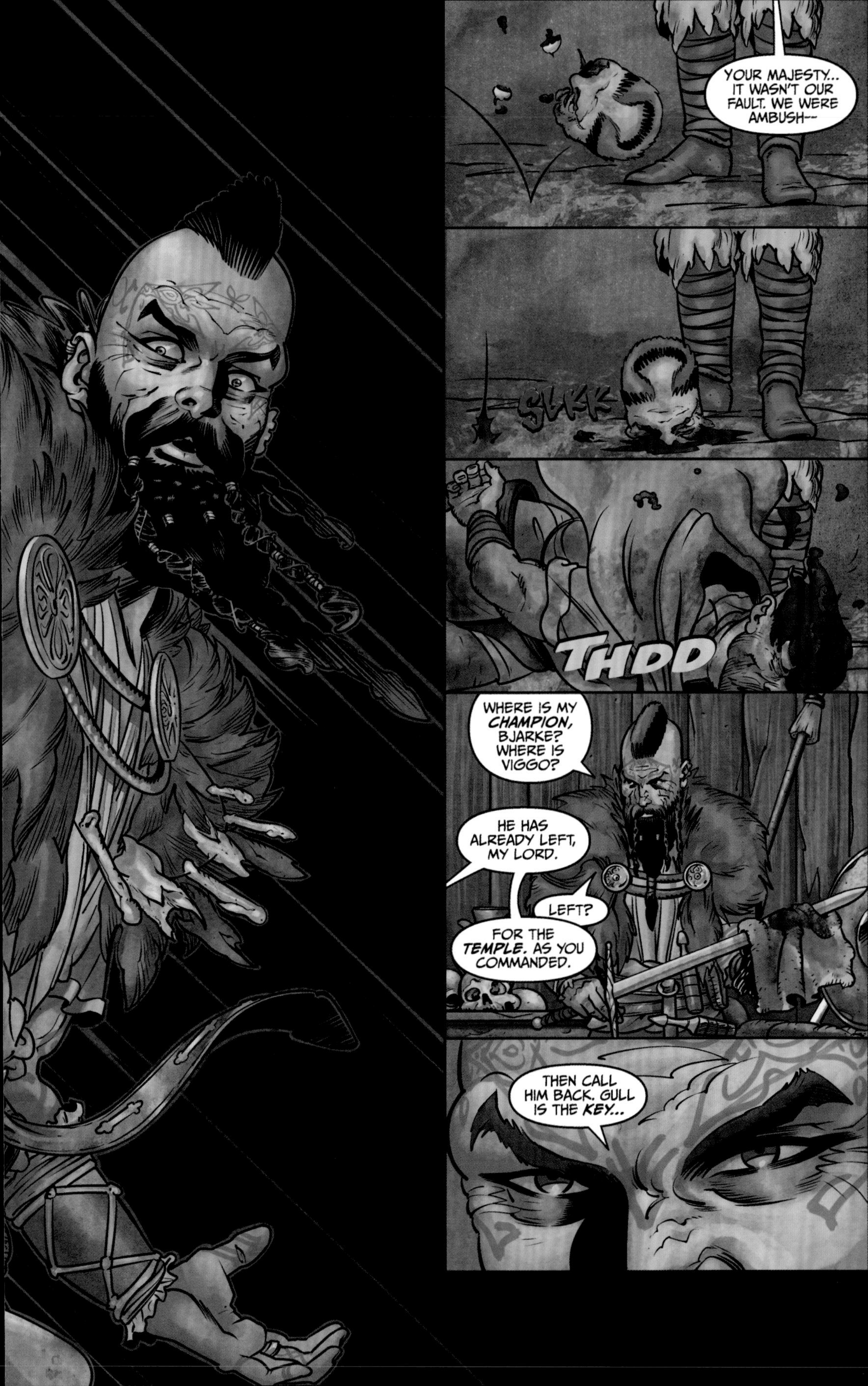
YOUR MAJESTY... IT WASN'T OUR FAULT. WE WERE AMBUSH--
SLKK
THDD
WHERE IS MY *CHAMPION*, BJARKE? WHERE IS VIGGO?
HE HAS ALREADY LEFT, MY LORD.
LEFT?
FOR THE *TEMPLE*. AS YOU COMMANDED.
THEN CALL HIM BACK. GULL IS THE *KEY*...

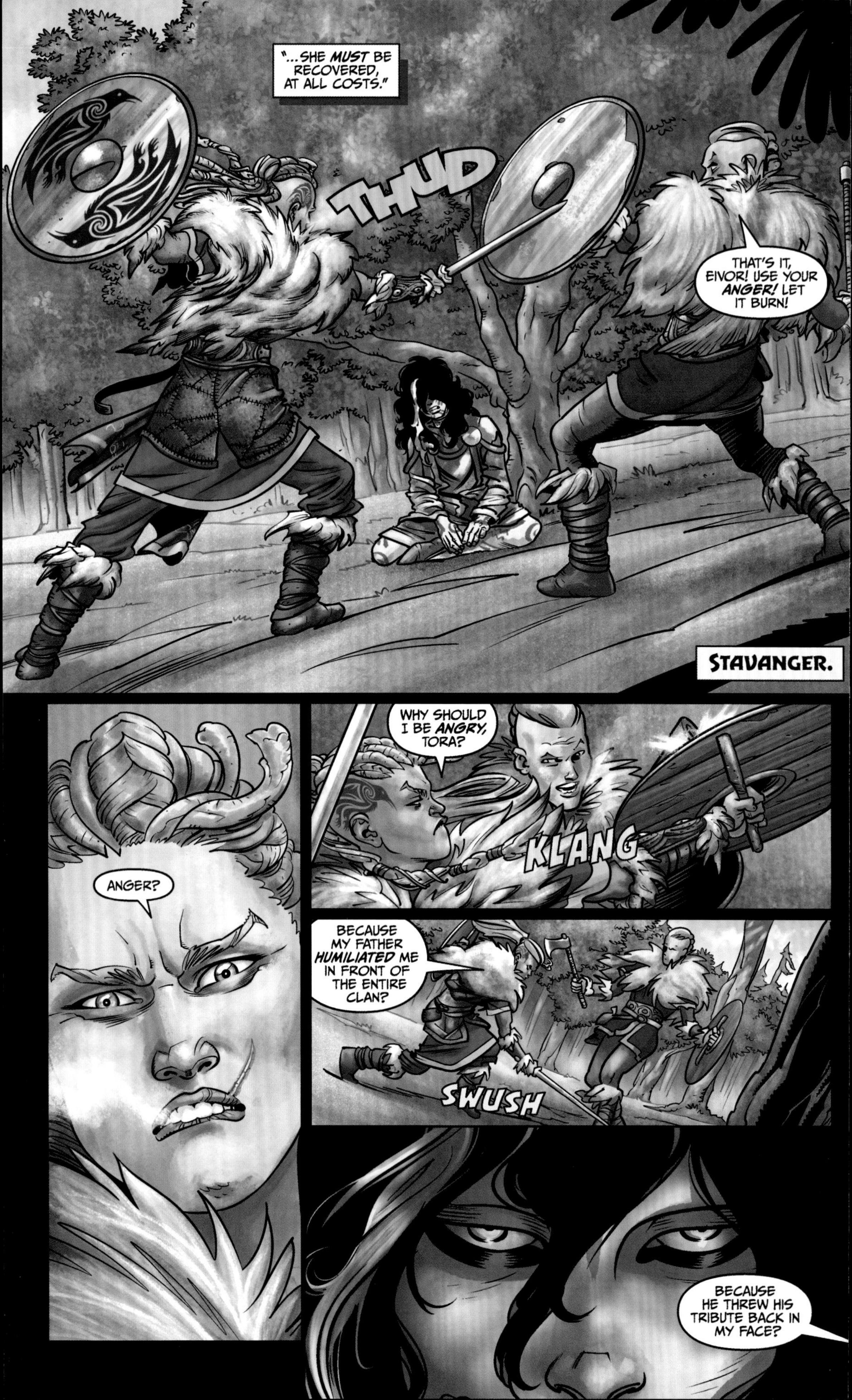
"...SHE MUST BE RECOVERED, AT ALL COSTS."
THUD
THAT'S IT, EIVOR! USE YOUR ANGER! LET IT BURN!
STAVANGER.
ANGER?
WHY SHOULD I BE ANGRY, TORA?
KLANG
BECAUSE MY FATHER HUMILIATED ME IN FRONT OF THE ENTIRE CLAN?
SWUSH
BECAUSE HE THREW HIS TRIBUTE BACK IN MY FACE?

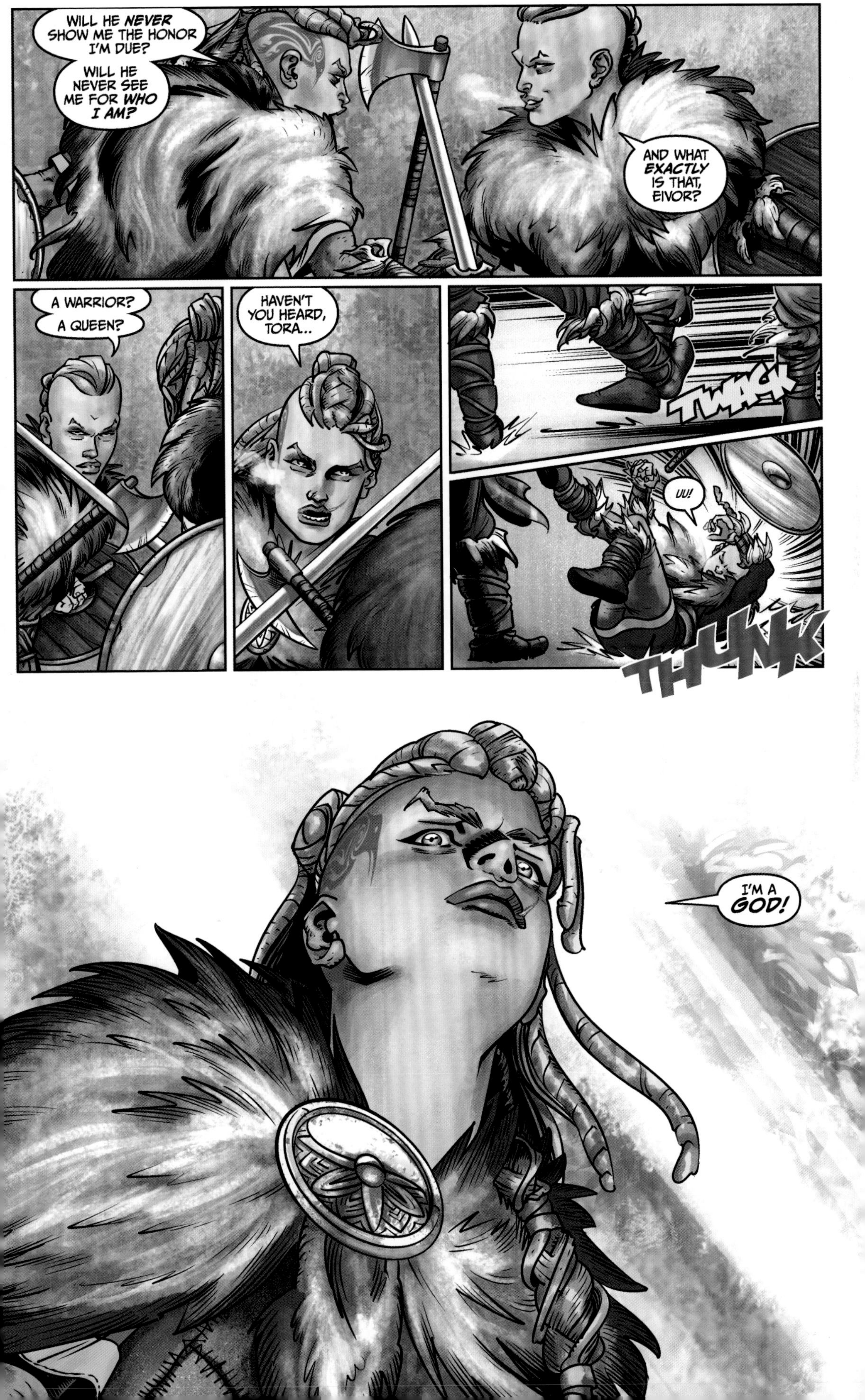
WILL HE NEVER SHOW ME THE HONOR I'M DUE?
WILL HE NEVER SEE ME FOR WHO I AM?
AND WHAT EXACTLY IS THAT, EIVOR?
A WARRIOR?
A QUEEN?
HAVEN'T YOU HEARD, TORA...
TWACK
UU!
THUNK
I'M A GOD!

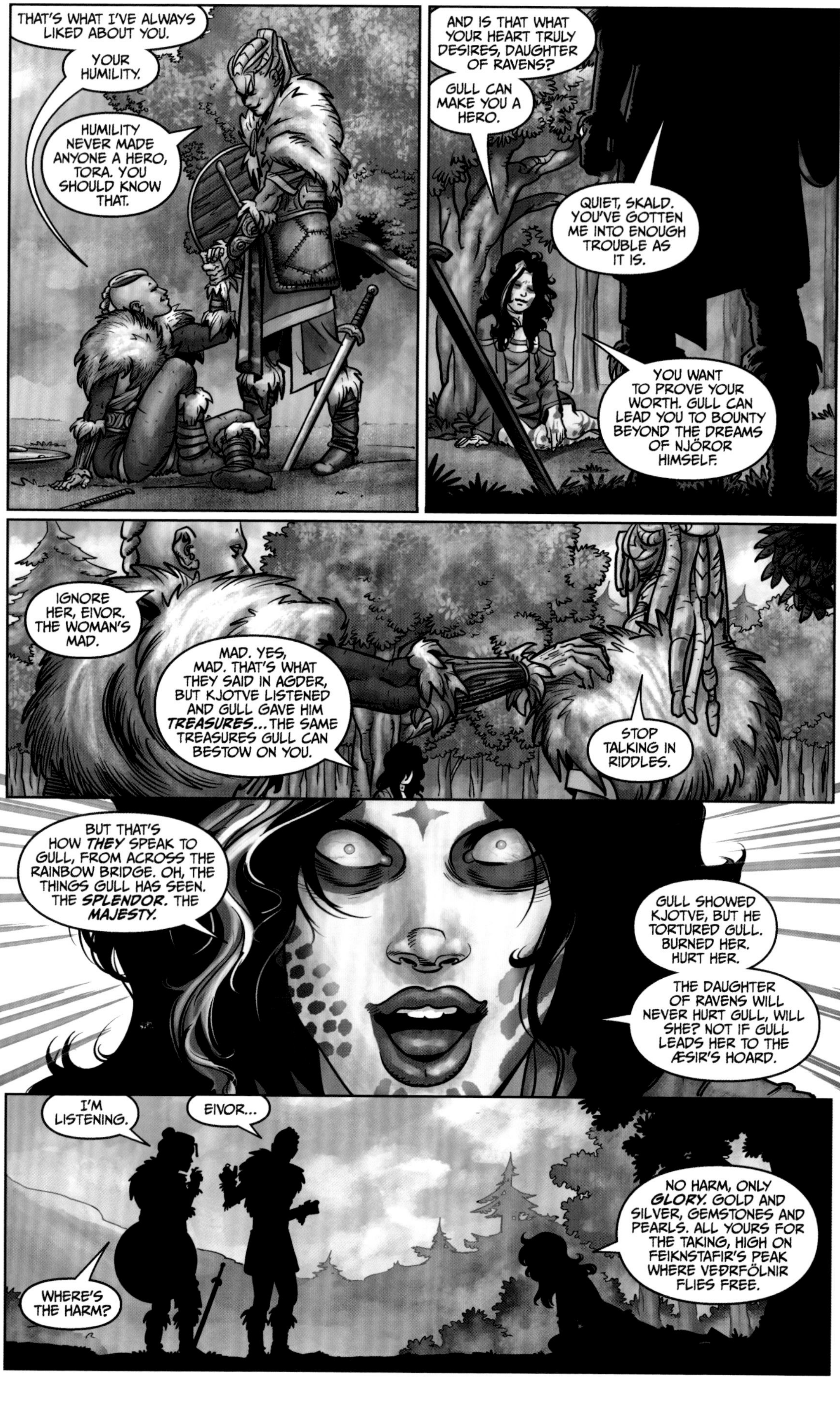

THAT'S WHAT I'VE ALWAYS LIKED ABOUT YOU.
YOUR HUMILITY.
HUMILITY NEVER MADE ANYONE A HERO, TORA. YOU SHOULD KNOW THAT.
AND IS THAT WHAT YOUR HEART TRULY DESIRES, DAUGHTER OF RAVENS?
GULL CAN MAKE YOU A HERO.
QUIET, SKALD. YOU'VE GOTTEN ME INTO ENOUGH TROUBLE AS IT IS.
YOU WANT TO PROVE YOUR WORTH. GULL CAN LEAD YOU TO BOUNTY BEYOND THE DREAMS OF NJÖROR HIMSELF.
IGNORE HER, EIVOR. THE WOMAN'S MAD.
MAD. YES, MAD. THAT'S WHAT THEY SAID IN AGDER, BUT KJOTVE LISTENED AND GULL GAVE HIM TREASURES... THE SAME TREASURES GULL CAN BESTOW ON YOU.
STOP TALKING IN RIDDLES.
BUT THAT'S HOW THEY SPEAK TO GULL, FROM ACROSS THE RAINBOW BRIDGE. OH, THE THINGS GULL HAS SEEN. THE SPLENDOR. THE MAJESTY.
GULL SHOWED KJOTVE, BUT HE TORTURED GULL. BURNED HER. HURT HER.
THE DAUGHTER OF RAVENS WILL NEVER HURT GULL, WILL SHE? NOT IF GULL LEADS HER TO THE ÆSIR'S HOARD.
I'M LISTENING.
EIVOR...
WHERE'S THE HARM?
NO HARM, ONLY GLORY. GOLD AND SILVER, GEMSTONES AND PEARLS. ALL YOURS FOR THE TAKING, HIGH ON FEIKNSTAFIR'S PEAK WHERE VEÐRFÖLNIR FLIES FREE.

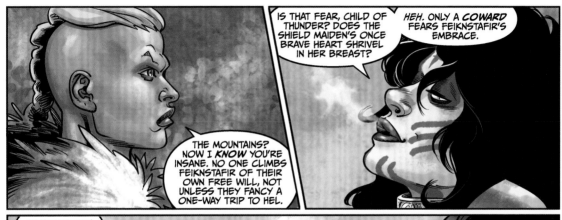

IS THAT FEAR, CHILD OF THUNDER? DOES THE SHIELD MAIDEN'S ONCE BRAVE HEART SHRIVEL IN HER BREAST?

HEH. ONLY A *COWARD* FEARS FEIKNSTAFIR'S EMBRACE.

THE MOUNTAINS? NOW I *KNOW* YOU'RE INSANE. NO ONE CLIMBS FEIKNSTAFIR OF THEIR OWN FREE WILL, NOT UNLESS THEY FANCY A ONE-WAY TRIP TO HEL.

WHAT DID YOU CALL ME?

TORA, DON'T.

IF THE WOMAN CAN LEAD ME TO THIS HOARD...

AS I HAVE SPOKEN, SO WILL IT BE. YOUR TREASURE. YOUR GLORY.

EIVOR, YOU CAN'T.

DON'T YOU SEE? THIS IS WHAT I'VE BEEN WAITING FOR. THE CHANCE TO SHOW MY FATHER WHAT I'M CAPABLE OF, WHO I TRULY AM. I *HAVE* TO DO THIS.

BUT THE KING--

DOESN'T NEED TO KNOW. NOT YET.

IF YOU WON'T JOIN ME, WILL YOU AT LEAST KEEP MY SECRET UNTIL I RETURN?

I DON'T KNOW. WHAT WOULD YOUR BROTHER SAY?

SIGURD? SIGURD ISN'T HERE, TORA.

HE'S OFF, HUGINN KNOWS WHERE, FORGING HIS OWN LEGEND--

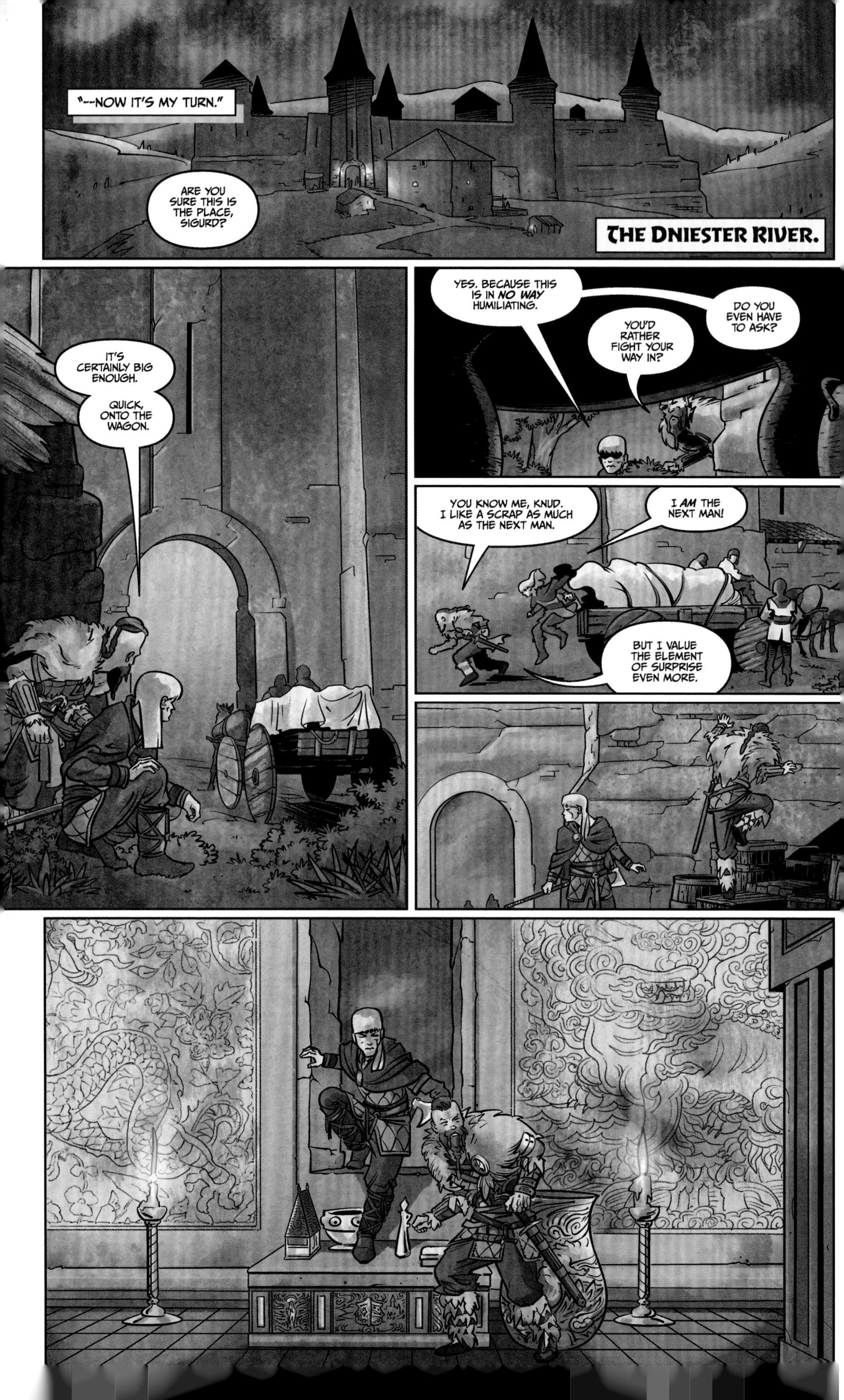
"--NOW IT'S MY TURN."
ARE YOU SURE THIS IS THE PLACE, SIGURD?
THE DNIESTER RIVER.
IT'S CERTAINLY BIG ENOUGH.
QUICK, ONTO THE WAGON.
YES. BECAUSE THIS IS IN NO WAY HUMILIATING.
YOU'D RATHER FIGHT YOUR WAY IN?
DO YOU EVEN HAVE TO ASK?
YOU KNOW ME, KNUD. I LIKE A SCRAP AS MUCH AS THE NEXT MAN.
I AM THE NEXT MAN!
BUT I VALUE THE ELEMENT OF SURPRISE EVEN MORE.

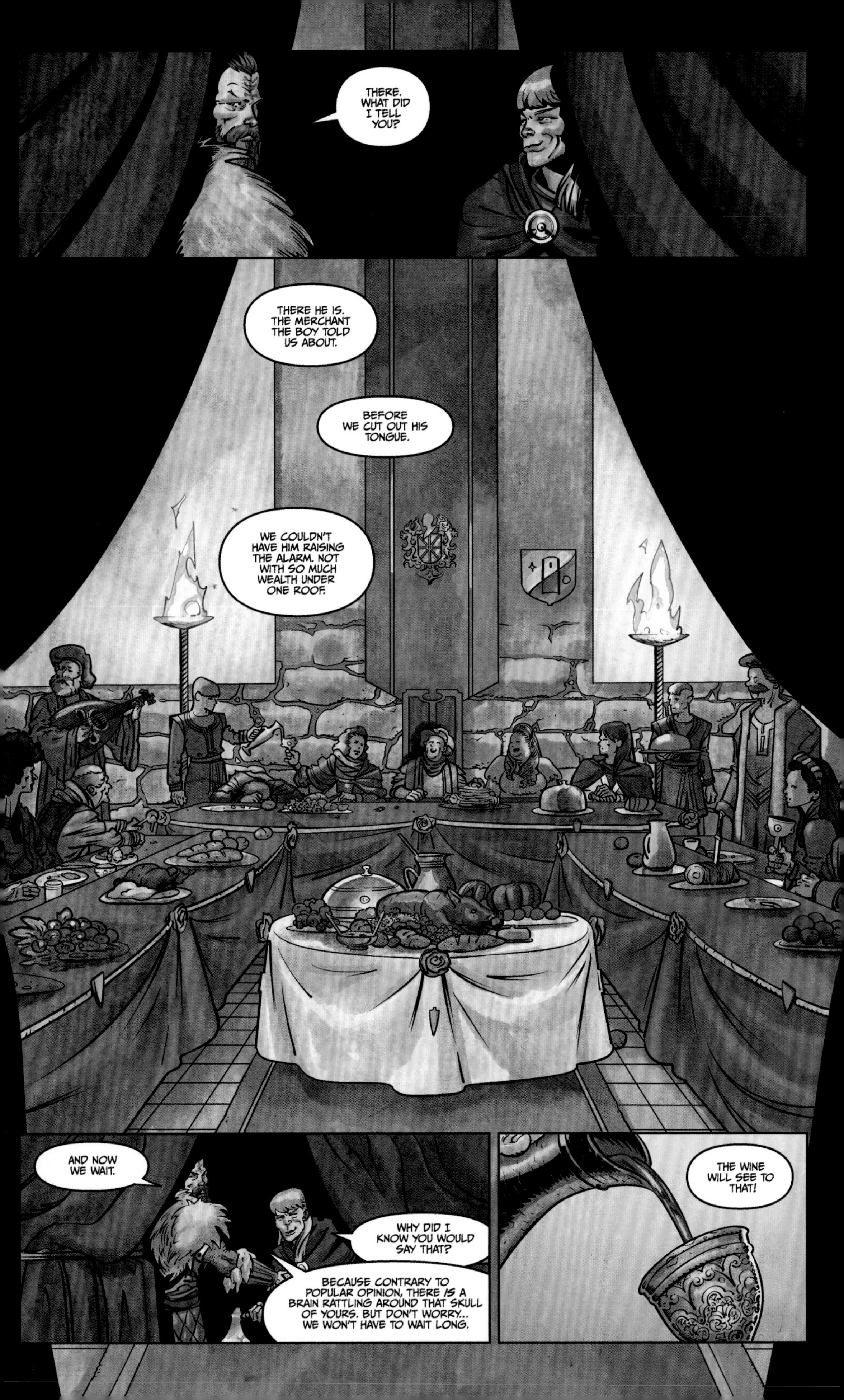
THERE. WHAT DID I TELL YOU?
THERE HE IS. THE MERCHANT THE BOY TOLD US ABOUT.
BEFORE WE CUT OUT HIS TONGUE.
WE COULDN'T HAVE HIM RAISING THE ALARM. NOT WITH SO MUCH WEALTH UNDER ONE ROOF.
AND NOW WE WAIT.
WHY DID I KNOW YOU WOULD SAY THAT?
BECAUSE CONTRARY TO POPULAR OPINION, THERE IS A BRAIN RATTLING AROUND THAT SKULL OF YOURS. BUT DON'T WORRY... WE WON'T HAVE TO WAIT LONG.
THE WINE WILL SEE TO THAT!

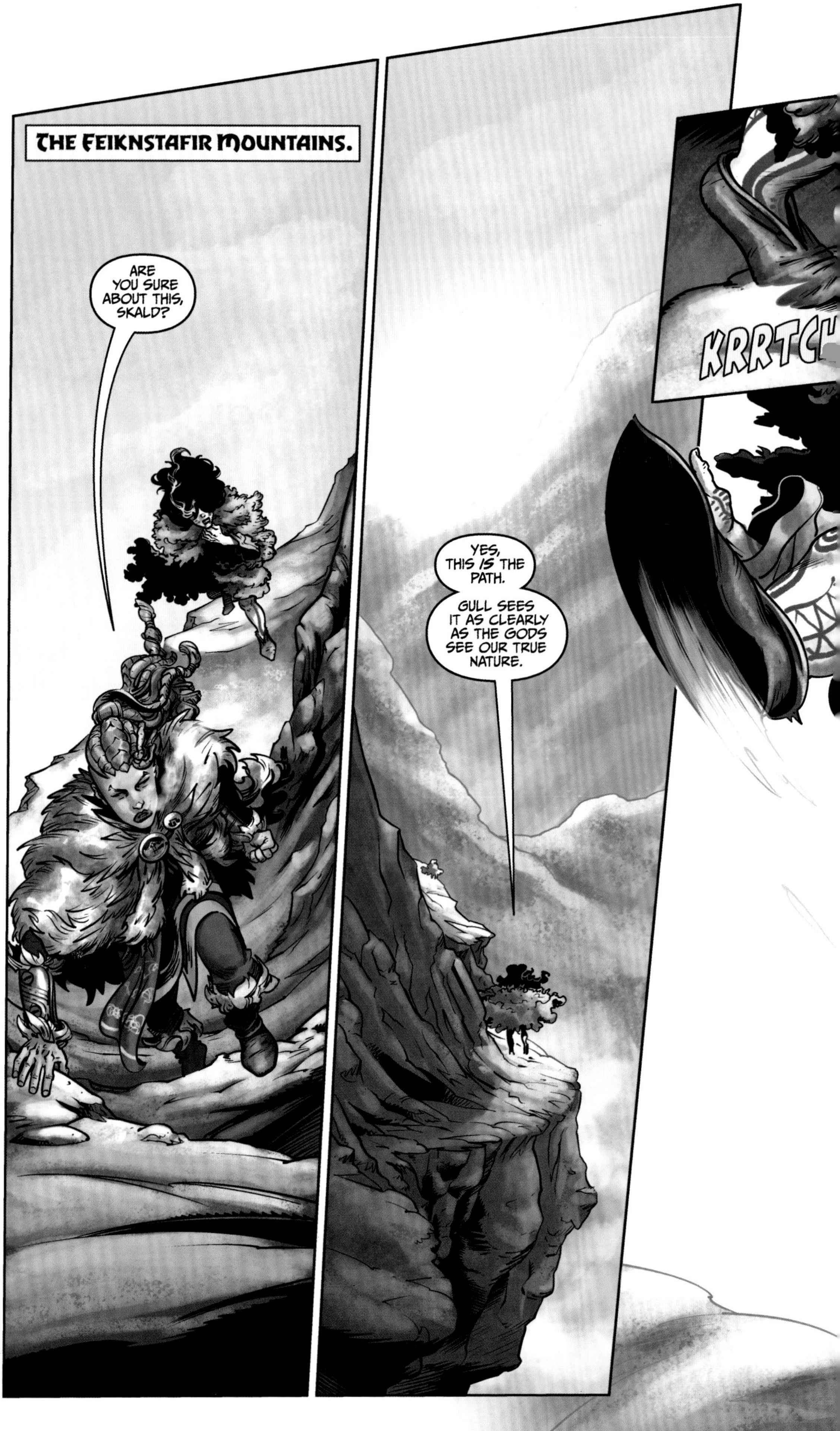
THE FEIKNSTAFIR MOUNTAINS.
ARE YOU SURE ABOUT THIS, SKALD?
YES, THIS *IS* THE PATH.
GULL SEES IT AS CLEARLY AS THE GODS SEE OUR TRUE NATURE.
KRRTCH

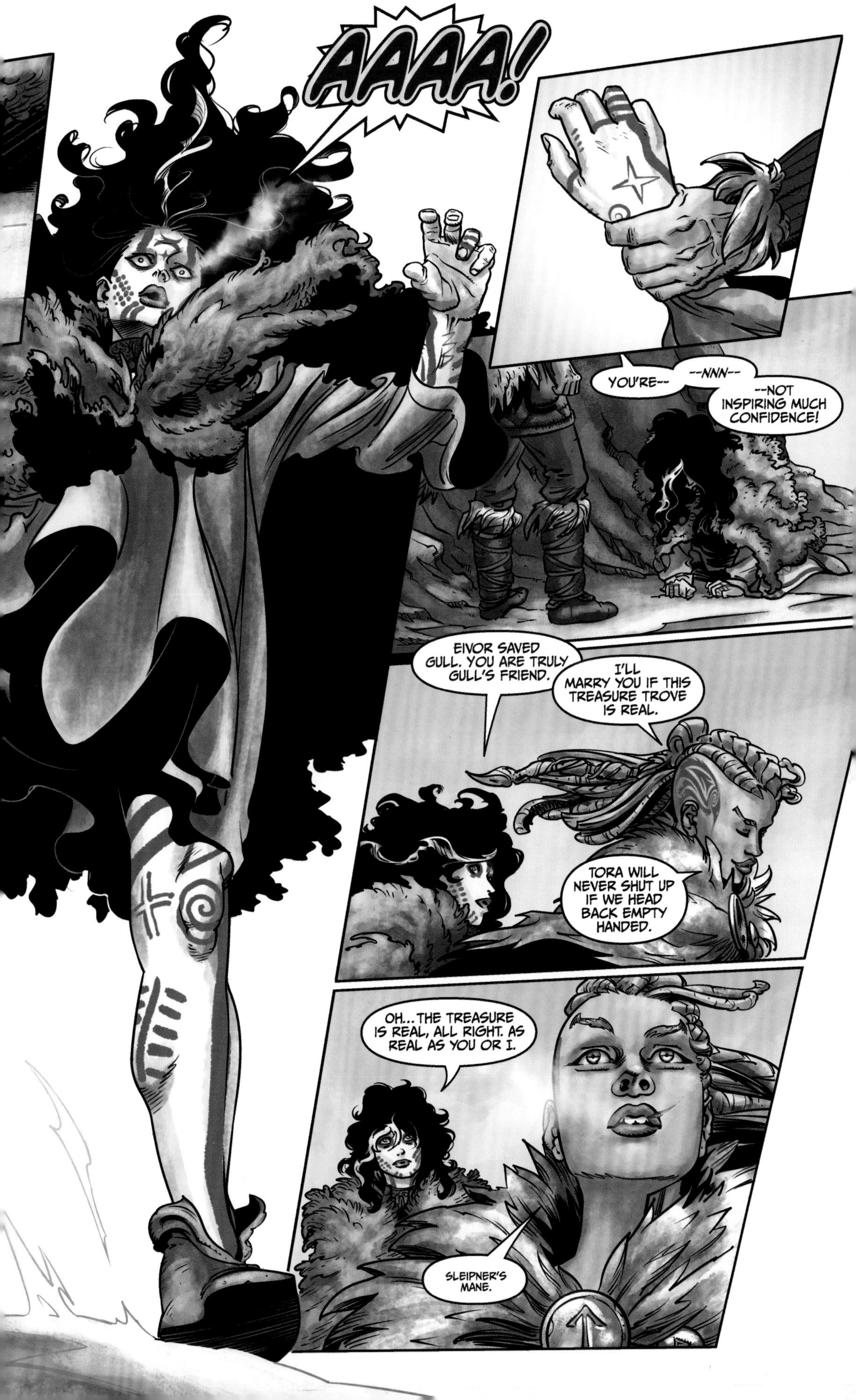
AAAA!
YOU'RE--
--NNN--
--NOT INSPIRING MUCH CONFIDENCE!
EIVOR SAVED GULL. YOU ARE TRULY GULL'S FRIEND.
I'LL MARRY YOU IF THIS TREASURE TROVE IS REAL.
TORA WILL NEVER SHUT UP IF WE HEAD BACK EMPTY HANDED.
OH...THE TREASURE IS REAL, ALL RIGHT. AS REAL AS YOU OR I.
SLEIPNER'S MANE.

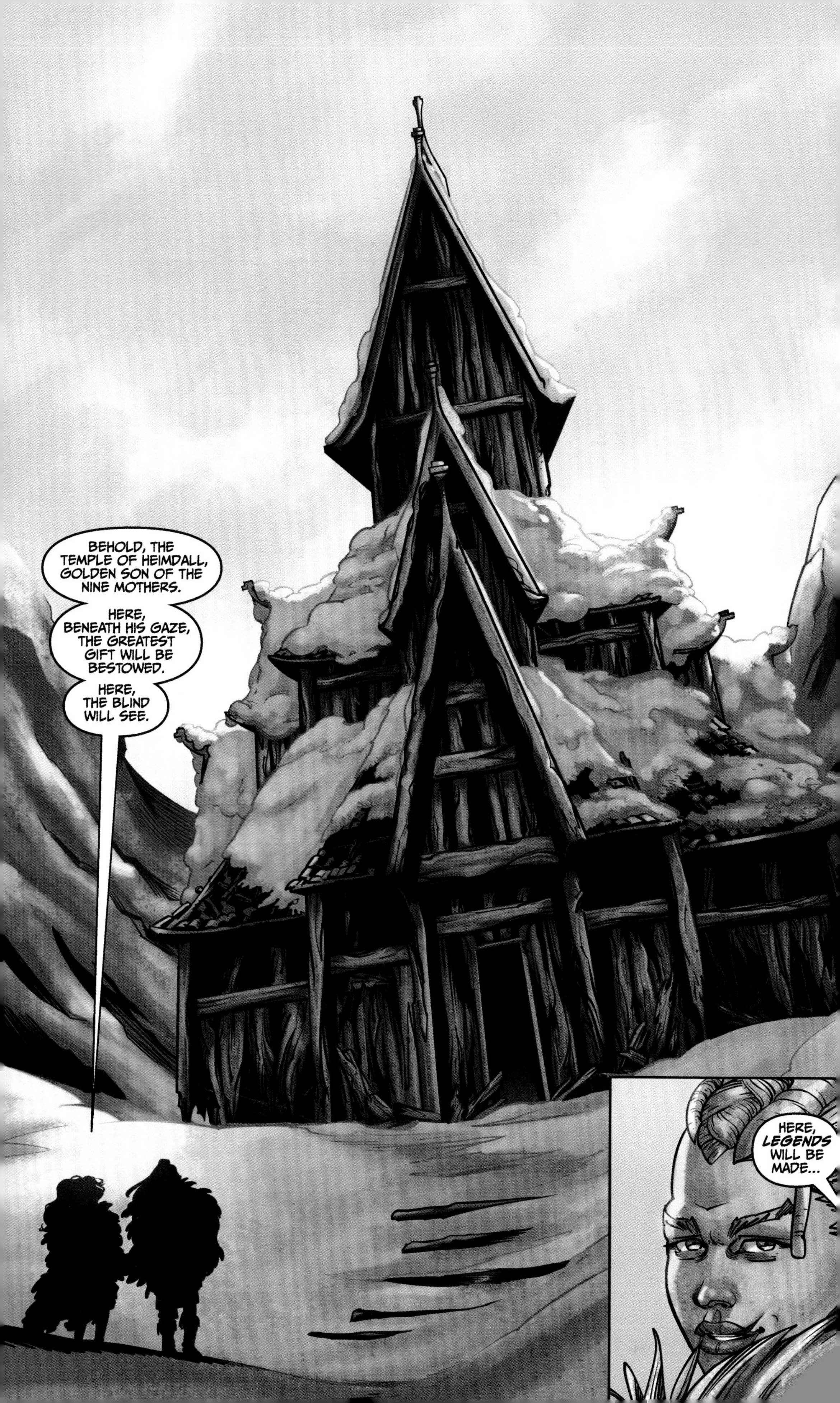
BEHOLD, THE TEMPLE OF HEIMDALL, GOLDEN SON OF THE NINE MOTHERS.
HERE, BENEATH HIS GAZE, THE GREATEST GIFT WILL BE BESTOWED.
HERE, THE BLIND WILL SEE.
HERE, *LEGENDS* WILL BE MADE...

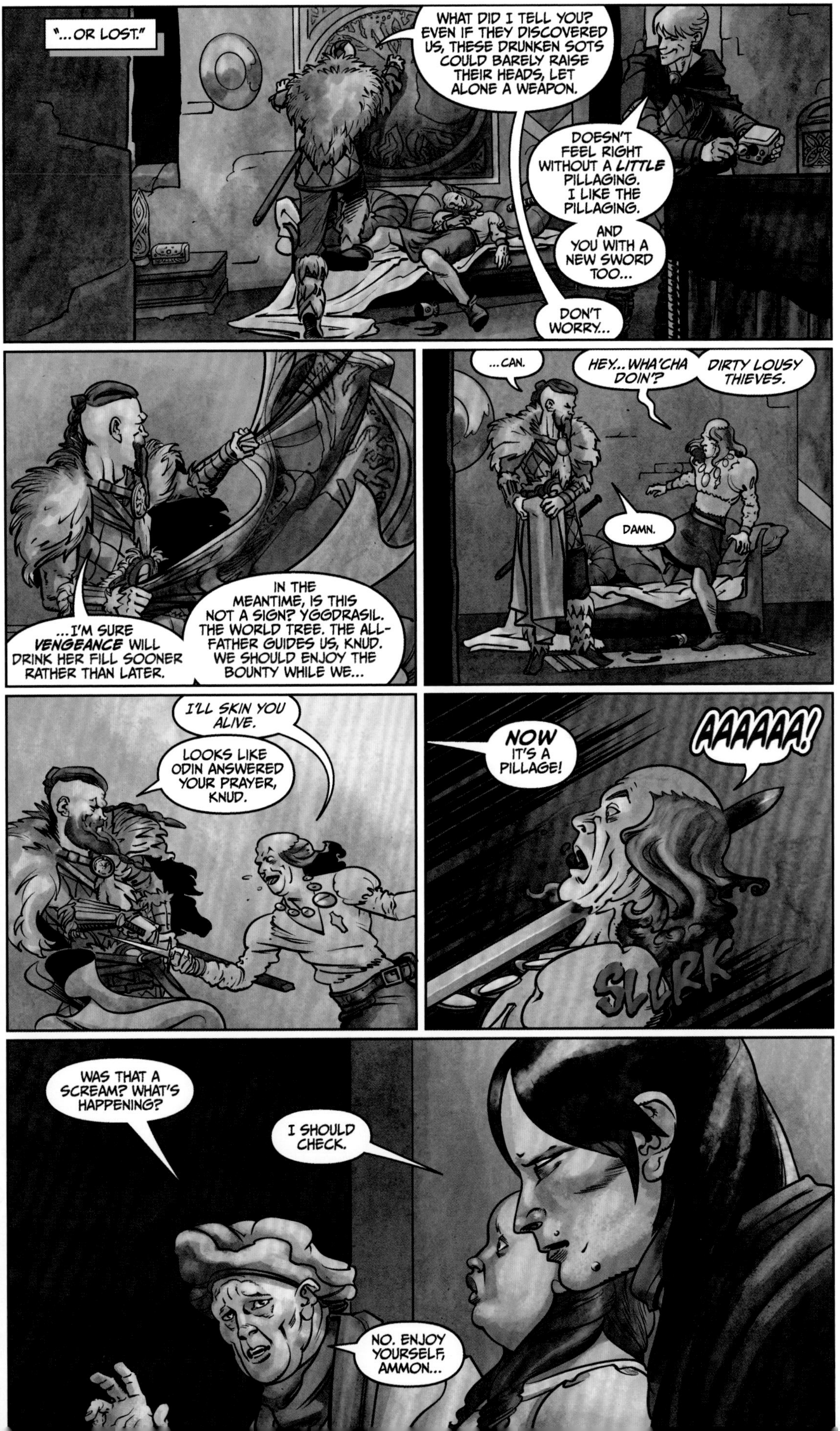
"...OR LOST."
WHAT DID I TELL YOU? EVEN IF THEY DISCOVERED US, THESE DRUNKEN SOTS COULD BARELY RAISE THEIR HEADS, LET ALONE A WEAPON.
DOESN'T FEEL RIGHT WITHOUT A *LITTLE* PILLAGING. I LIKE THE PILLAGING.
AND YOU WITH A NEW SWORD TOO...
DON'T WORRY...
...I'M SURE *VENGEANCE* WILL DRINK HER FILL SOONER RATHER THAN LATER.
IN THE MEANTIME, IS THIS NOT A SIGN? YGGDRASIL. THE WORLD TREE. THE ALL-FATHER GUIDES US, KNUD. WE SHOULD ENJOY THE BOUNTY WHILE WE...
...CAN.
HEY...WHA'CHA DOIN'?
DIRTY LOUSY THIEVES.
DAMN.
I'LL SKIN YOU ALIVE.
LOOKS LIKE ODIN ANSWERED YOUR PRAYER, KNUD.
NOW IT'S A PILLAGE!
AAAAAA!
SLURK
WAS THAT A SCREAM? WHAT'S HAPPENING?
I SHOULD CHECK.
NO. ENJOY YOURSELF, AMMON...

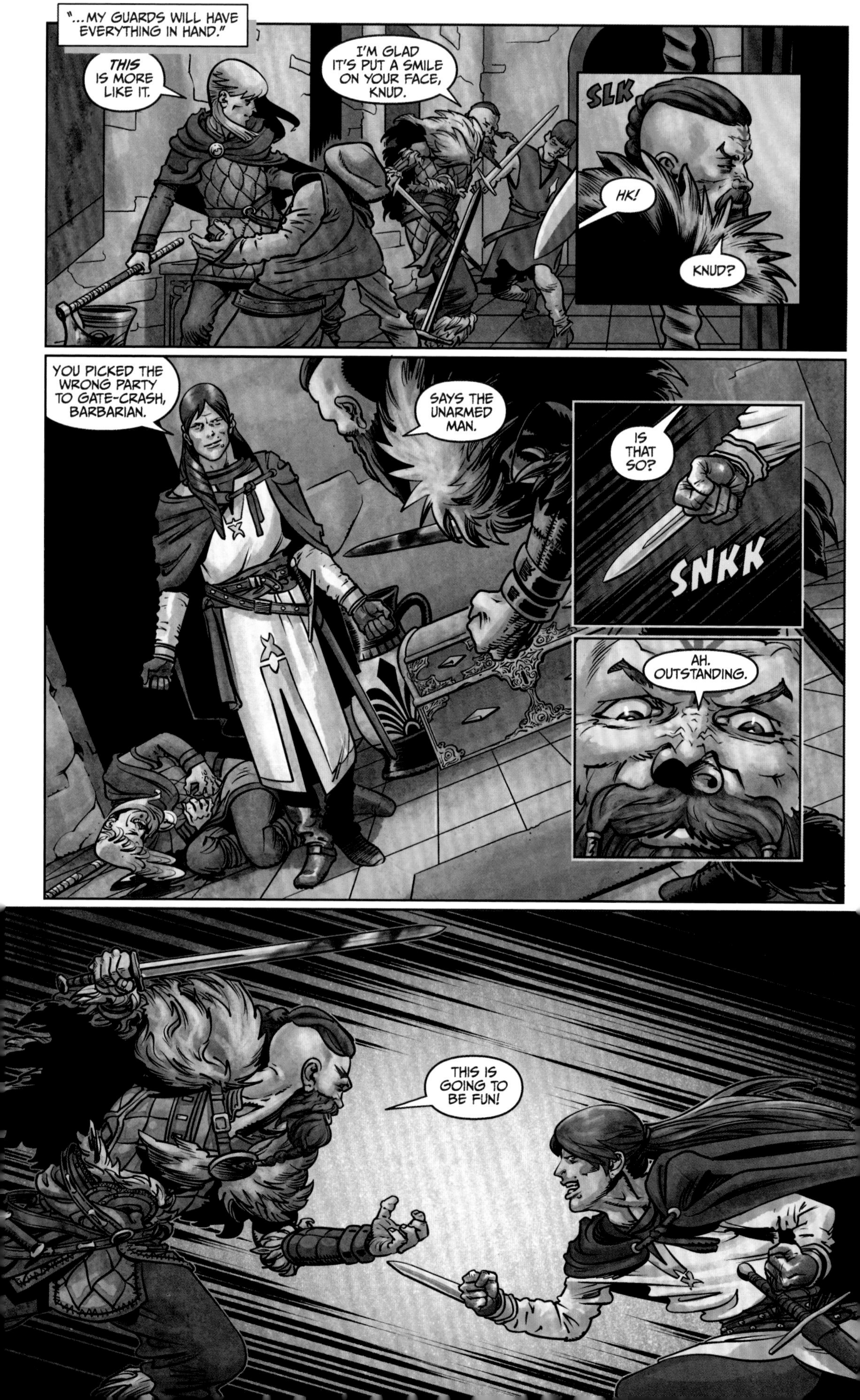

"...MY GUARDS WILL HAVE EVERYTHING IN HAND."
THIS IS MORE LIKE IT.
I'M GLAD IT'S PUT A SMILE ON YOUR FACE, KNUD.
SLK
HK!
KNUD?
YOU PICKED THE WRONG PARTY TO GATE-CRASH, BARBARIAN.
SAYS THE UNARMED MAN.
IS THAT SO?
SNKK
AH. OUTSTANDING.
THIS IS GOING TO BE FUN!

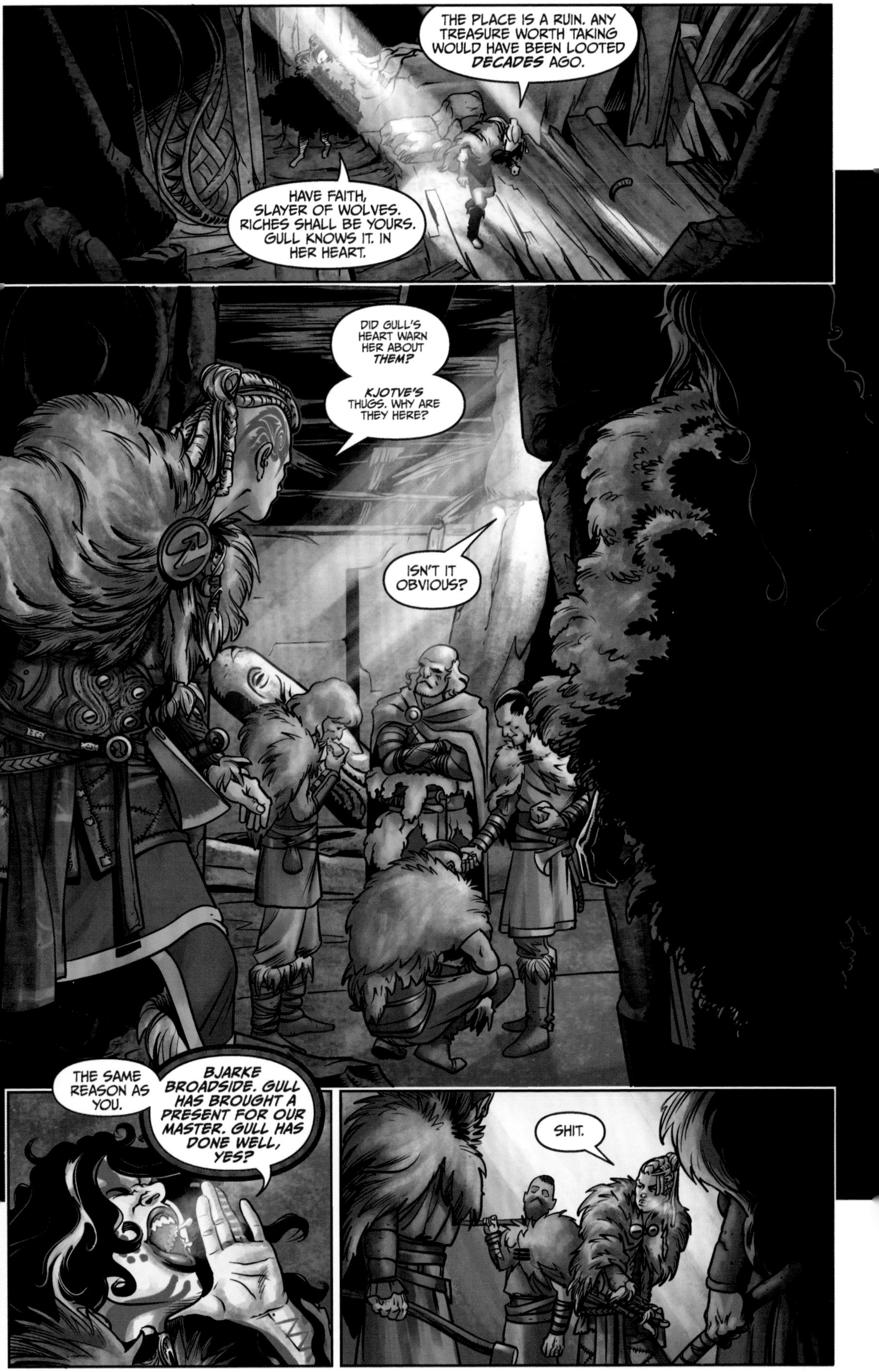
THE PLACE IS A RUIN. ANY TREASURE WORTH TAKING WOULD HAVE BEEN LOOTED *DECADES* AGO.
HAVE FAITH, SLAYER OF WOLVES. RICHES SHALL BE YOURS. GULL KNOWS IT. IN HER HEART.
DID GULL'S HEART WARN HER ABOUT *THEM?*
KJOTVE'S THUGS. WHY ARE THEY HERE?
ISN'T IT OBVIOUS?
THE SAME REASON AS YOU.
BJARKE BROADSIDE. GULL HAS BROUGHT A PRESENT FOR OUR MASTER. GULL HAS DONE WELL, YES?
SHIT.

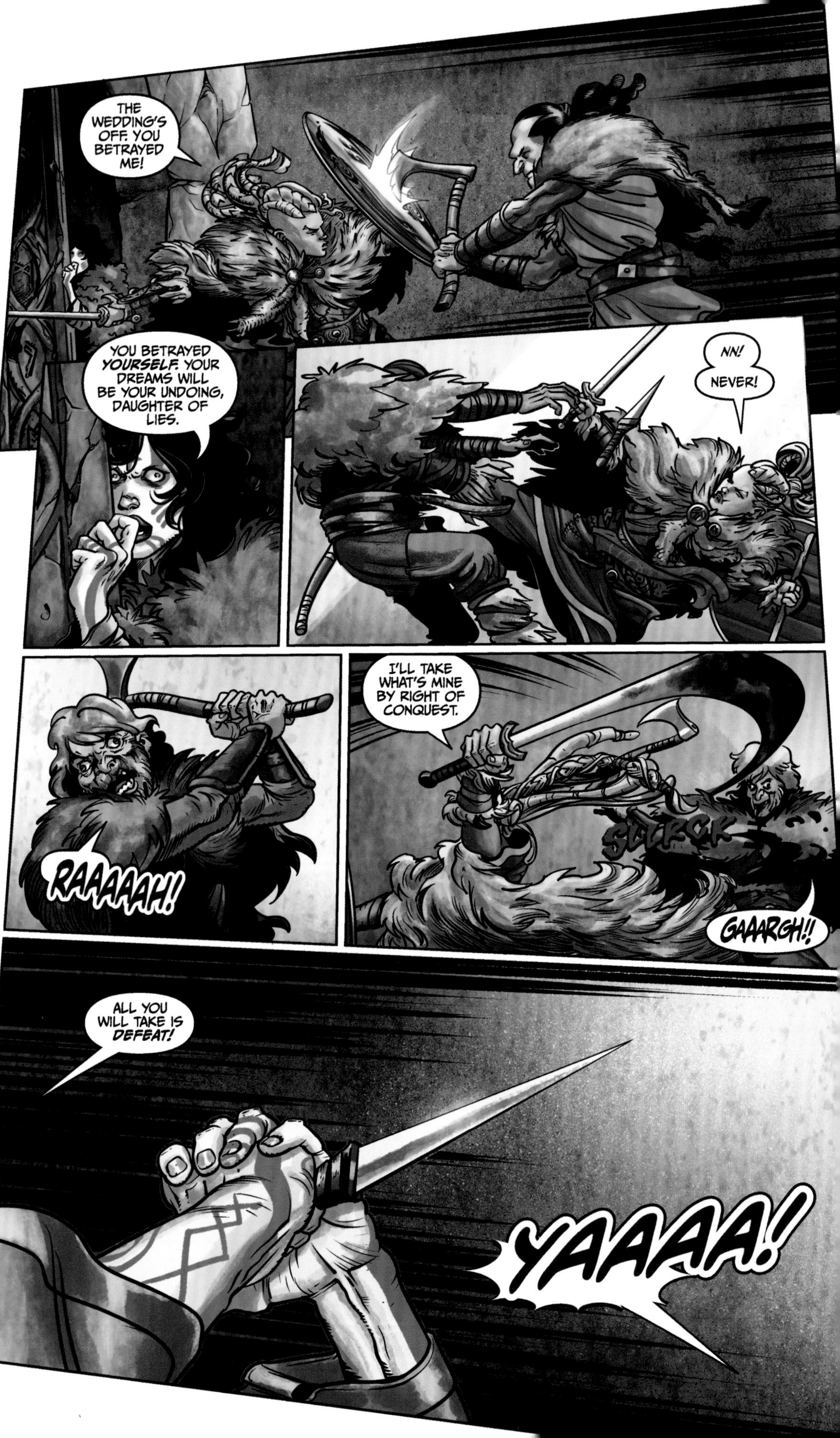
THE WEDDING'S OFF. YOU BETRAYED ME!
YOU BETRAYED *YOURSELF.* YOUR DREAMS WILL BE YOUR UNDOING, DAUGHTER OF LIES.
NN!
NEVER!
RAAAAAH!
I'LL TAKE WHAT'S MINE BY RIGHT OF CONQUEST.
SLLRCK
GAAARGH!!
ALL YOU WILL TAKE IS *DEFEAT!*
YAAAA!

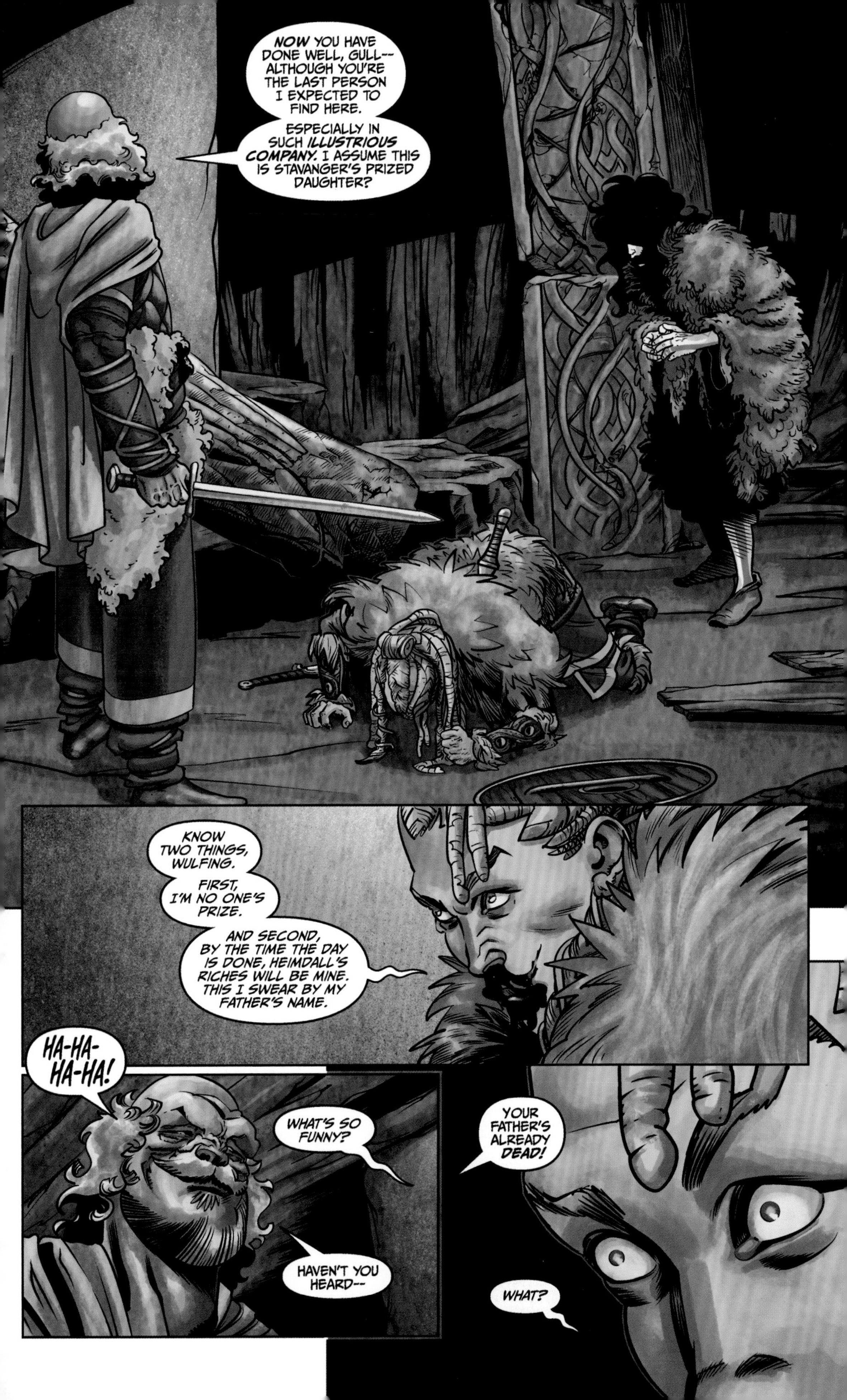
NOW YOU HAVE DONE WELL, GULL-- ALTHOUGH YOU'RE THE LAST PERSON I EXPECTED TO FIND HERE.
ESPECIALLY IN SUCH ILLUSTRIOUS COMPANY. I ASSUME THIS IS STAVANGER'S PRIZED DAUGHTER?
KNOW TWO THINGS, WULFING.
FIRST, I'M NO ONE'S PRIZE.
AND SECOND, BY THE TIME THE DAY IS DONE, HEIMDALL'S RICHES WILL BE MINE. THIS I SWEAR BY MY FATHER'S NAME.
HA-HA-HA-HA!
WHAT'S SO FUNNY?
HAVEN'T YOU HEARD--
YOUR FATHER'S ALREADY DEAD!
WHAT?

"NO!"

STAVANGER.

HKK!

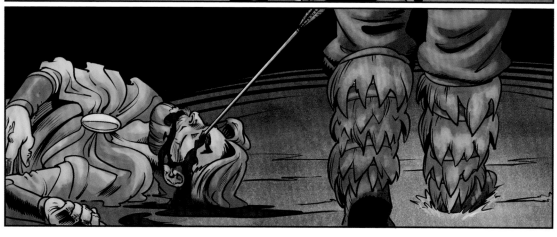

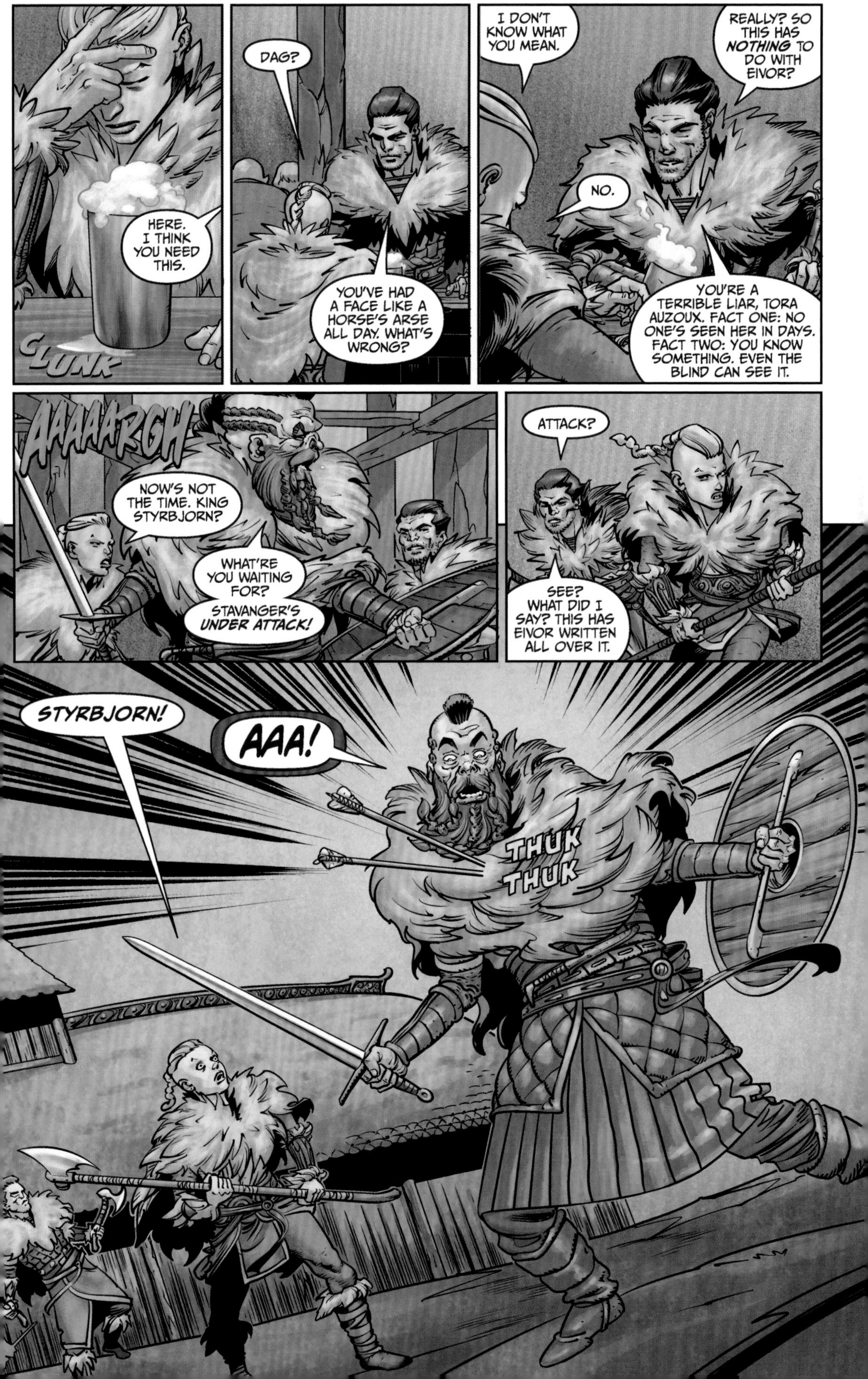
HERE. I THINK YOU NEED THIS.
CLUNK
DAG?
YOU'VE HAD A FACE LIKE A HORSE'S ARSE ALL DAY. WHAT'S WRONG?
I DON'T KNOW WHAT YOU MEAN.
REALLY? SO THIS HAS NOTHING TO DO WITH EIVOR?
NO.
YOU'RE A TERRIBLE LIAR, TORA AUZOUX. FACT ONE: NO ONE'S SEEN HER IN DAYS. FACT TWO: YOU KNOW SOMETHING. EVEN THE BLIND CAN SEE IT.
AAAAARGH
NOW'S NOT THE TIME. KING STYRBJORN?
WHAT'RE YOU WAITING FOR?
STAVANGER'S UNDER ATTACK!
ATTACK?
SEE? WHAT DID I SAY? THIS HAS EIVOR WRITTEN ALL OVER IT.
STYRBJORN!
AAA!
THUK
THUK

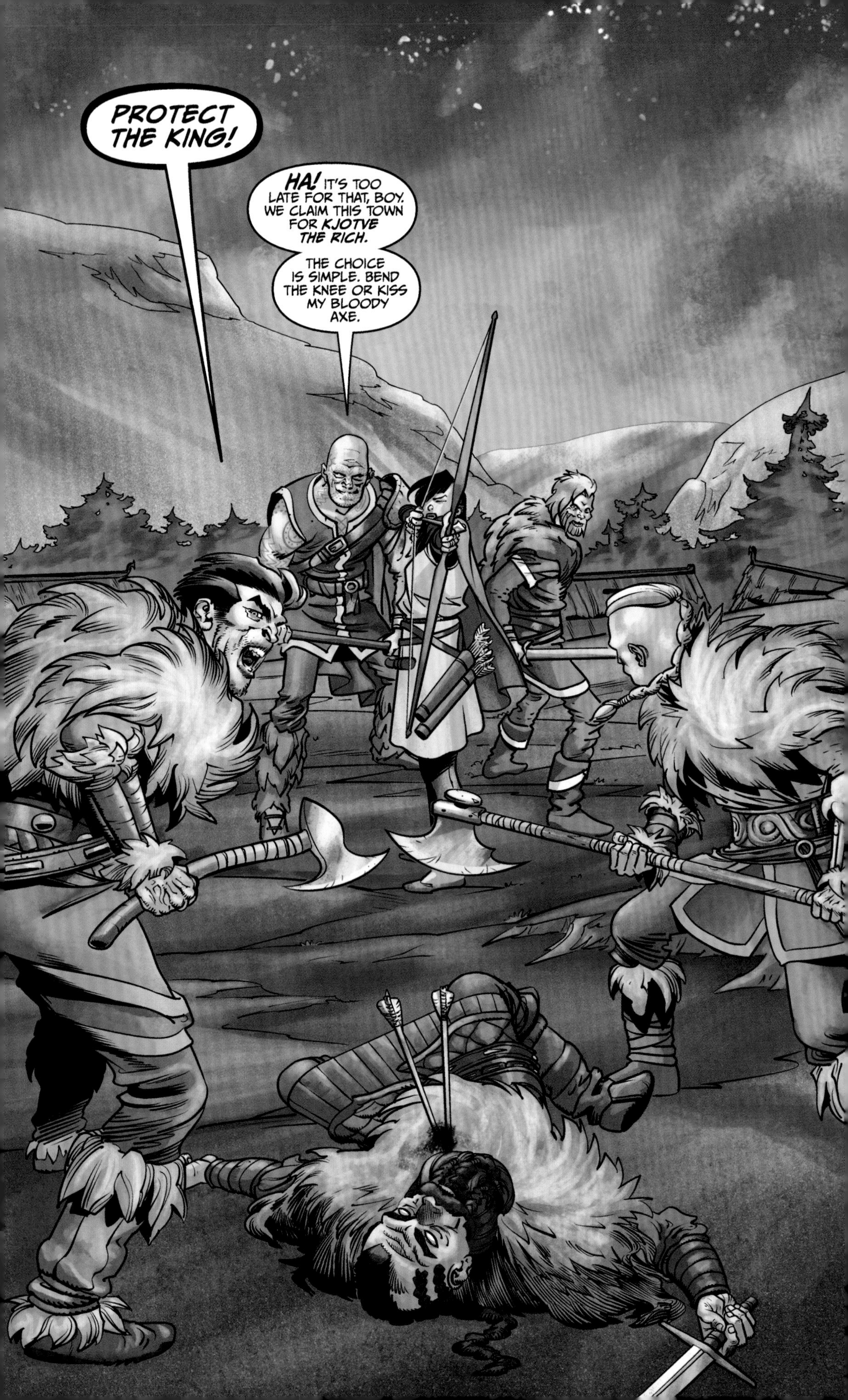
PROTECT THE KING!
HA! IT'S TOO LATE FOR THAT, BOY. WE CLAIM THIS TOWN FOR KJOTVE THE RICH.
THE CHOICE IS SIMPLE. BEND THE KNEE OR KISS MY BLOODY AXE.

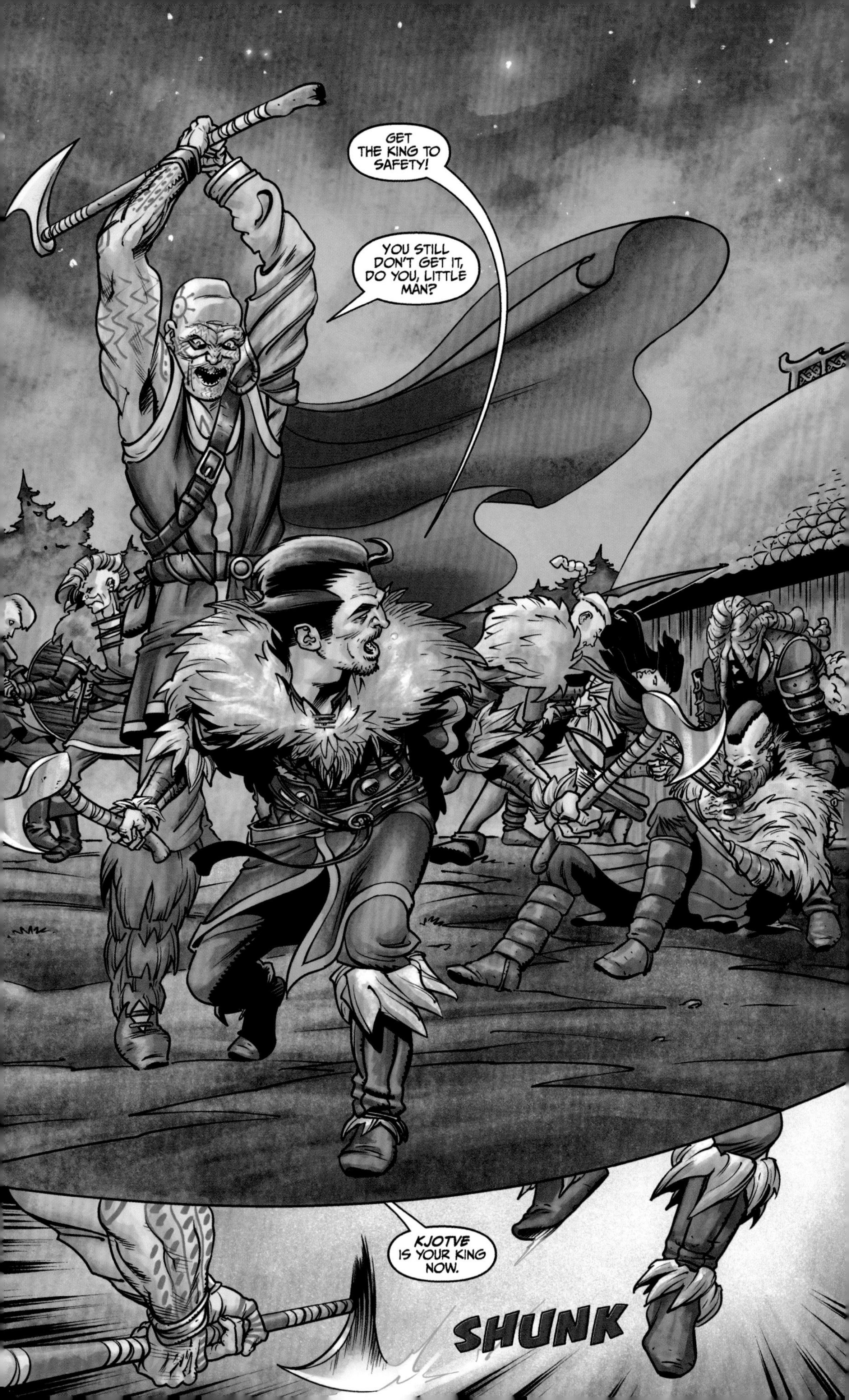
GET THE KING TO SAFETY!
YOU STILL DON'T GET IT, DO YOU, LITTLE MAN?
KJOTVE IS YOUR KING NOW.
SHUNK

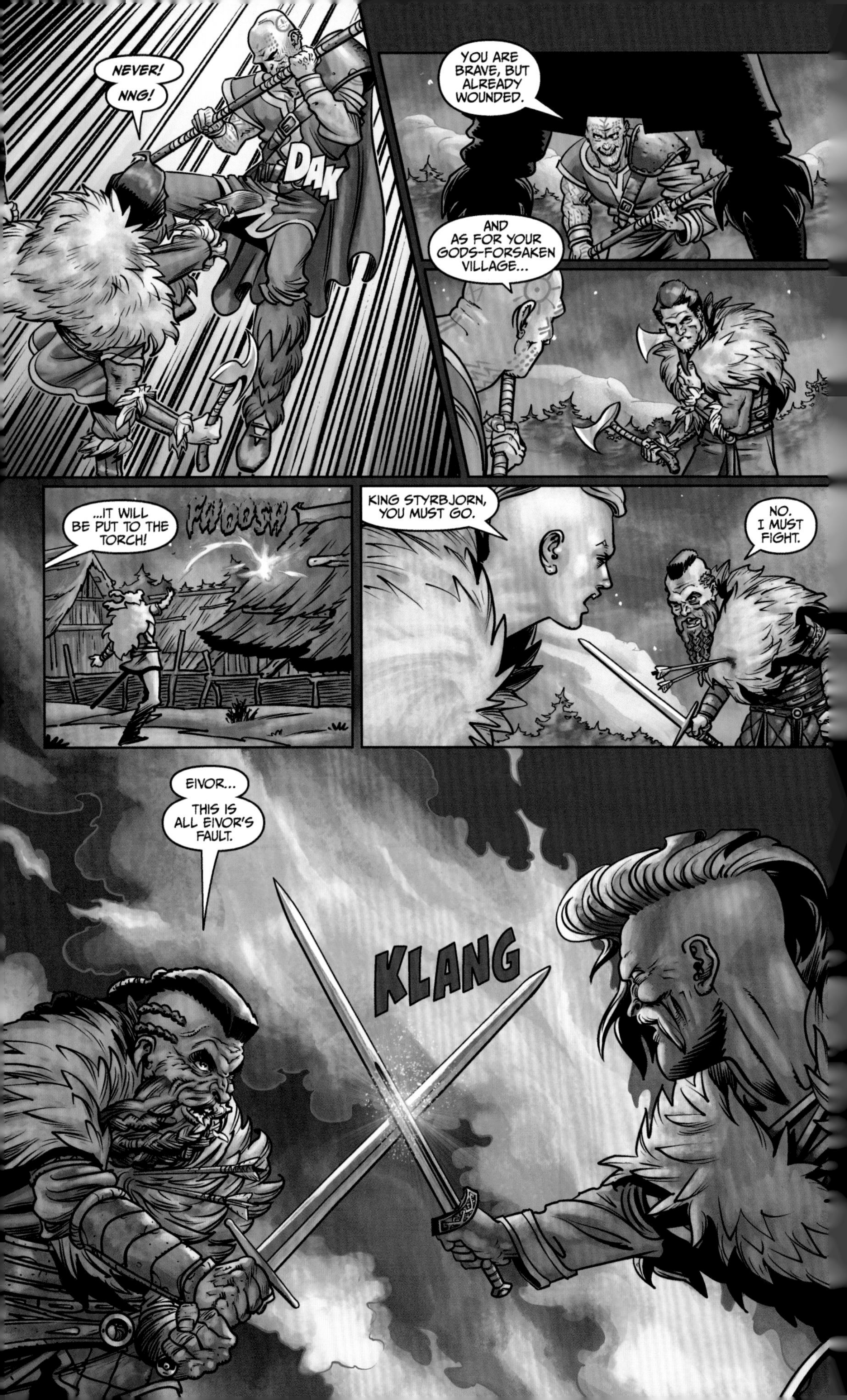
NEVER!
NNG!
DAK
YOU ARE BRAVE, BUT ALREADY WOUNDED.
AND AS FOR YOUR GODS-FORSAKEN VILLAGE...
...IT WILL BE PUT TO THE TORCH!
FWOOSH
KING STYRBJORN, YOU MUST GO.
NO. I MUST FIGHT.
EIVOR...
THIS IS ALL EIVOR'S FAULT.
KLANG

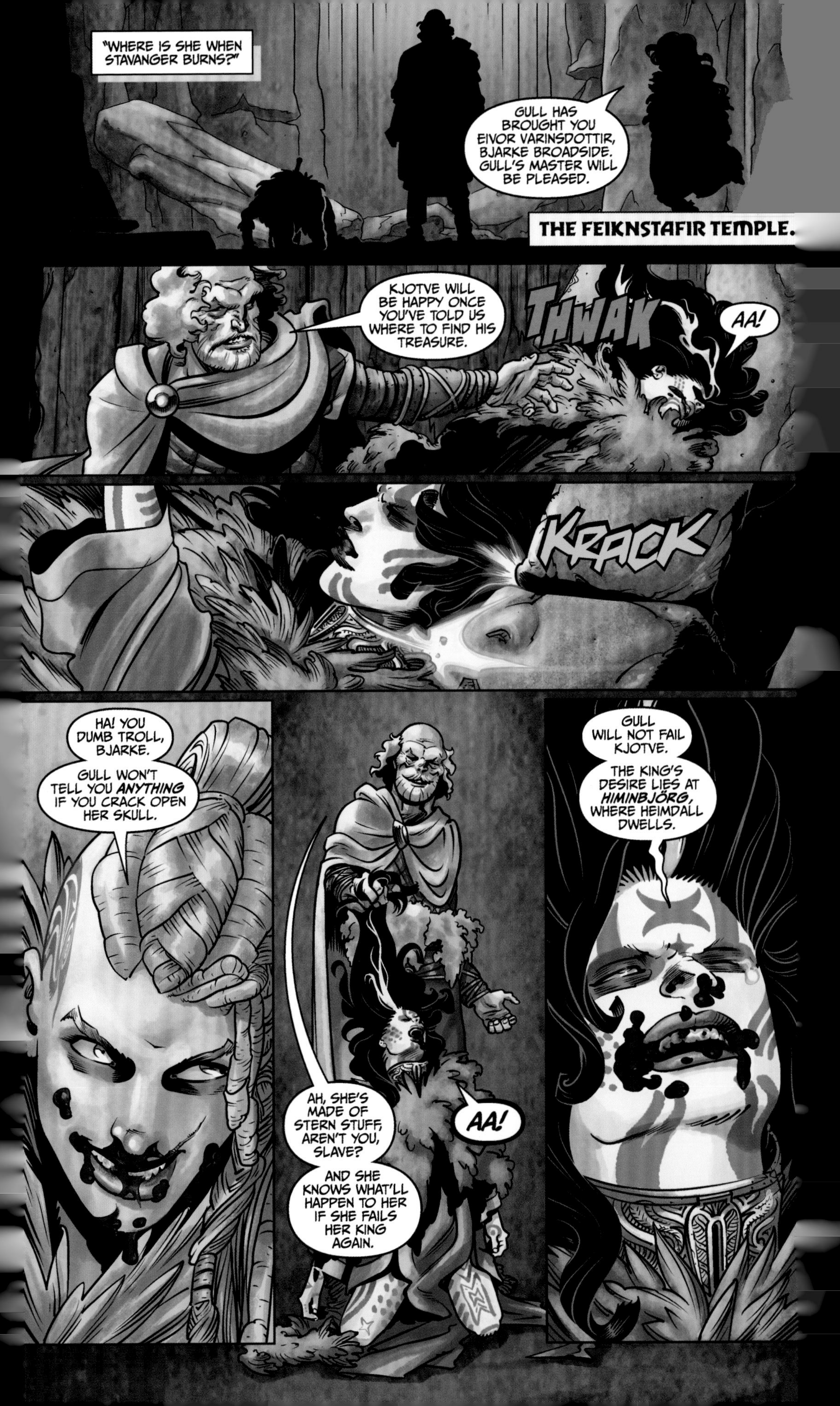
"WHERE IS SHE WHEN STAVANGER BURNS?"
GULL HAS BROUGHT YOU EIVOR VARINSDOTTIR, BJARKE BROADSIDE. GULL'S MASTER WILL BE PLEASED.
THE FEIKNSTAFIR TEMPLE.
KJOTVE WILL BE HAPPY ONCE YOU'VE TOLD US WHERE TO FIND HIS TREASURE.
THWAK
AA!
KRACK
HA! YOU DUMB TROLL, BJARKE.
GULL WON'T TELL YOU ANYTHING IF YOU CRACK OPEN HER SKULL.
AH, SHE'S MADE OF STERN STUFF, AREN'T YOU, SLAVE?
AND SHE KNOWS WHAT'LL HAPPEN TO HER IF SHE FAILS HER KING AGAIN.
AA!
GULL WILL NOT FAIL KJOTVE.
THE KING'S DESIRE LIES AT HIMINBJÖRG, WHERE HEIMDALL DWELLS.

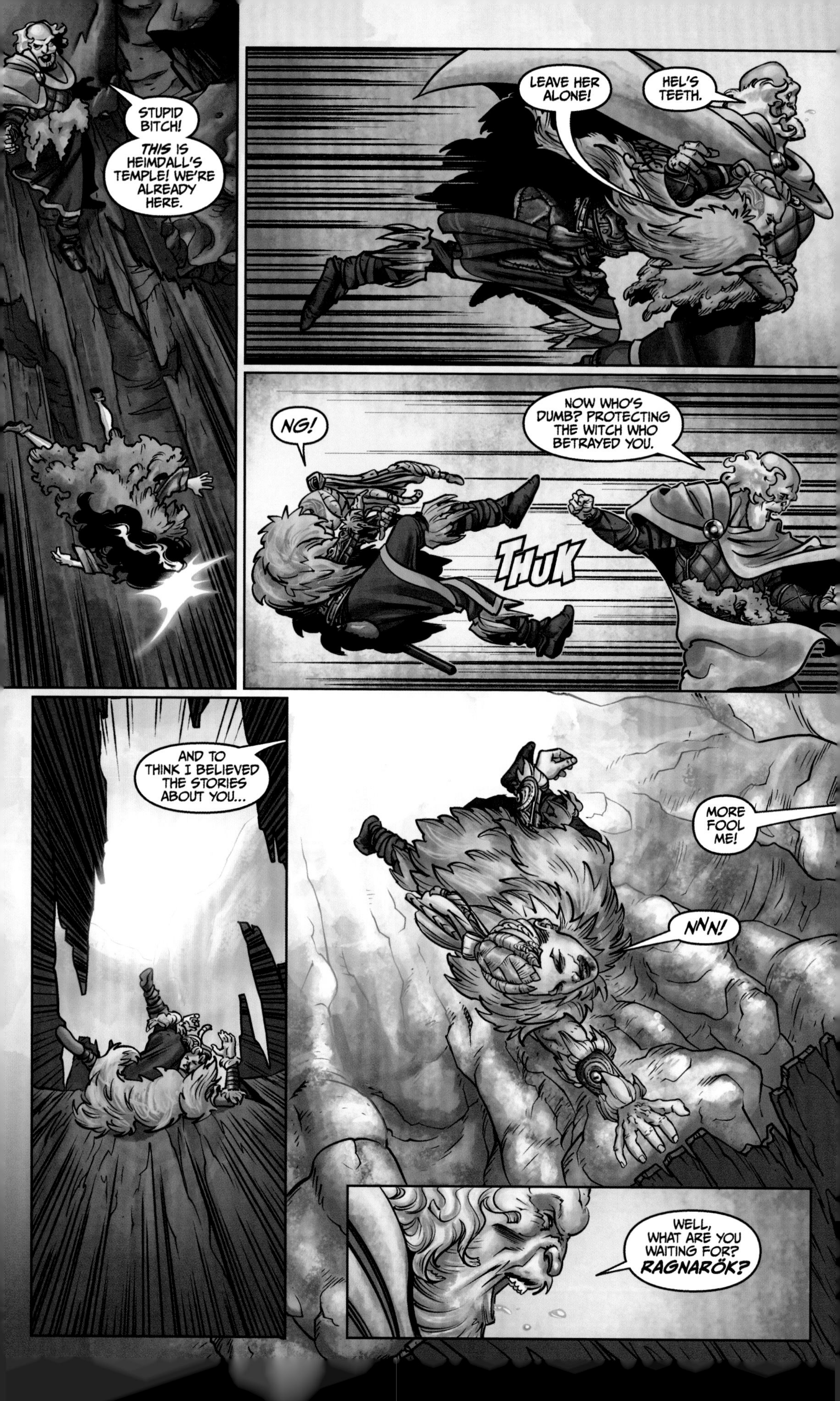
STUPID BITCH! THIS IS HEIMDALL'S TEMPLE! WE'RE ALREADY HERE.
LEAVE HER ALONE!
HEL'S TEETH.
NG!
NOW WHO'S DUMB? PROTECTING THE WITCH WHO BETRAYED YOU.
THUK
AND TO THINK I BELIEVED THE STORIES ABOUT YOU...
MORE FOOL ME!
NNN!
WELL, WHAT ARE YOU WAITING FOR? RAGNARÖK?

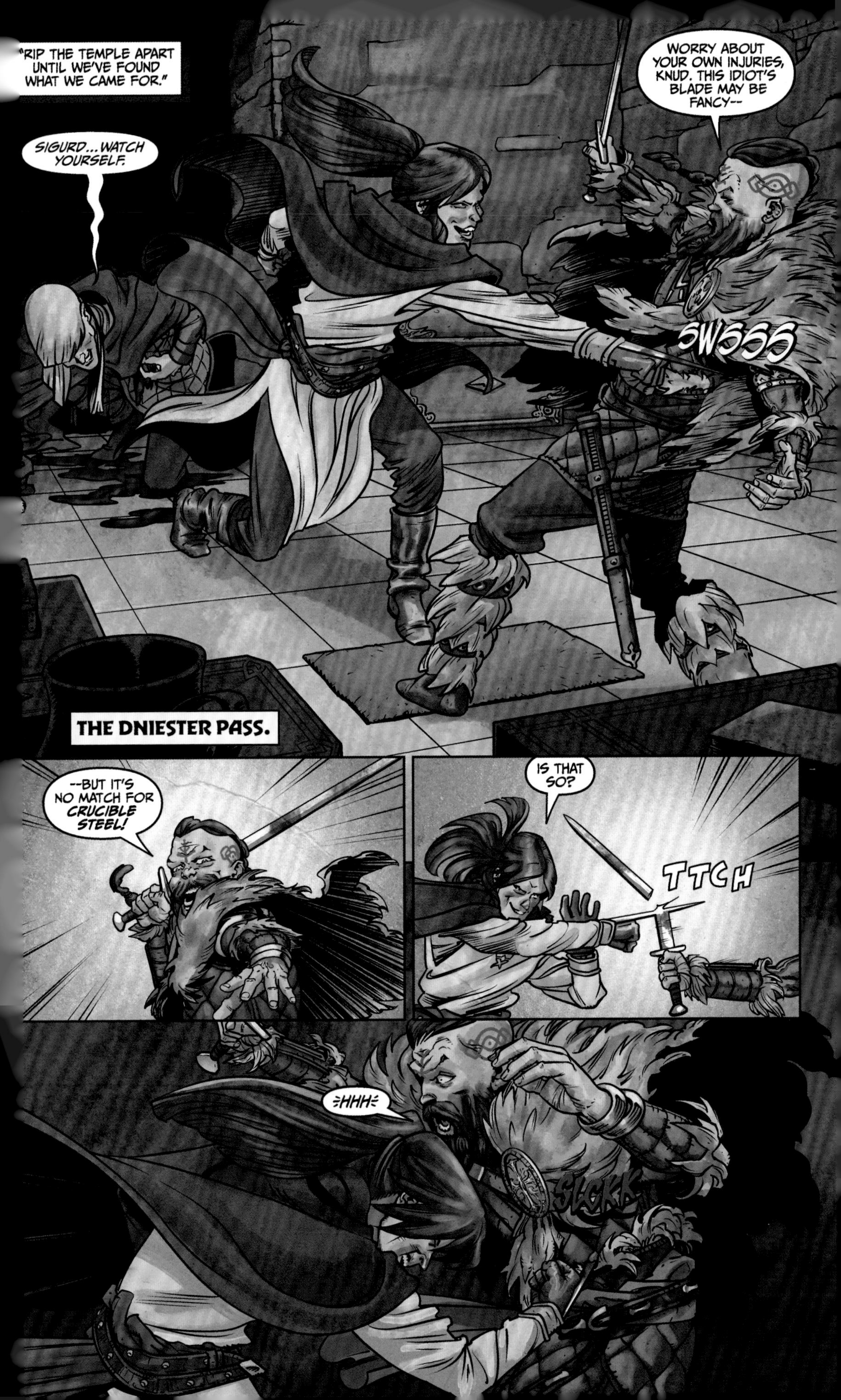
"RIP THE TEMPLE APART UNTIL WE'VE FOUND WHAT WE CAME FOR."
SIGURD... WATCH YOURSELF.
WORRY ABOUT YOUR OWN INJURIES, KNUD. THIS IDIOT'S BLADE MAY BE FANCY--
SWSSS
THE DNIESTER PASS.
--BUT IT'S NO MATCH FOR CRUCIBLE STEEL!
IS THAT SO?
TTCH
HHH
SLCKK

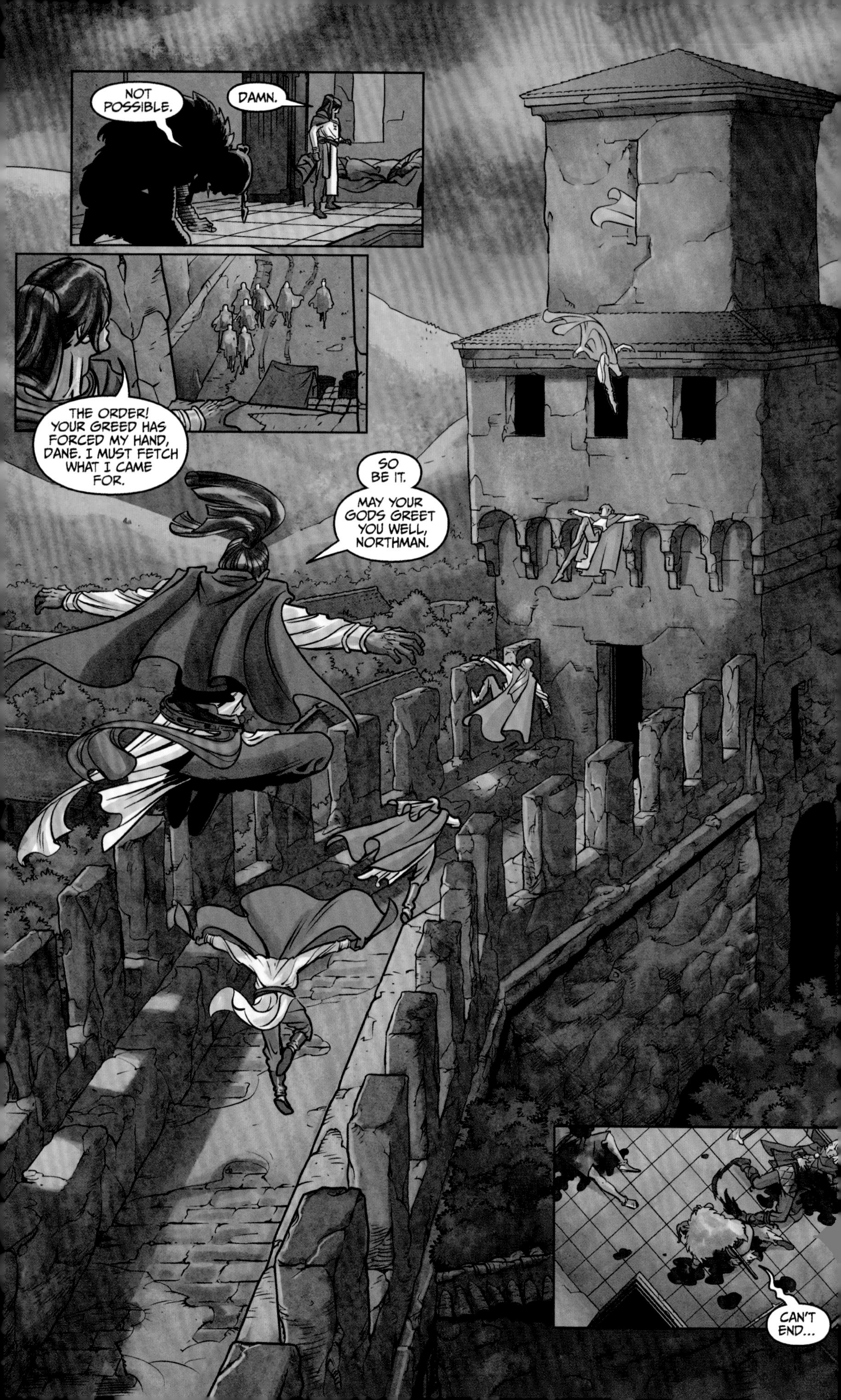
NOT POSSIBLE.
DAMN.
THE ORDER! YOUR GREED HAS FORCED MY HAND, DANE. I MUST FETCH WHAT I CAME FOR.
SO BE IT.
MAY YOUR GODS GREET YOU WELL, NORTHMAN.
CAN'T END...

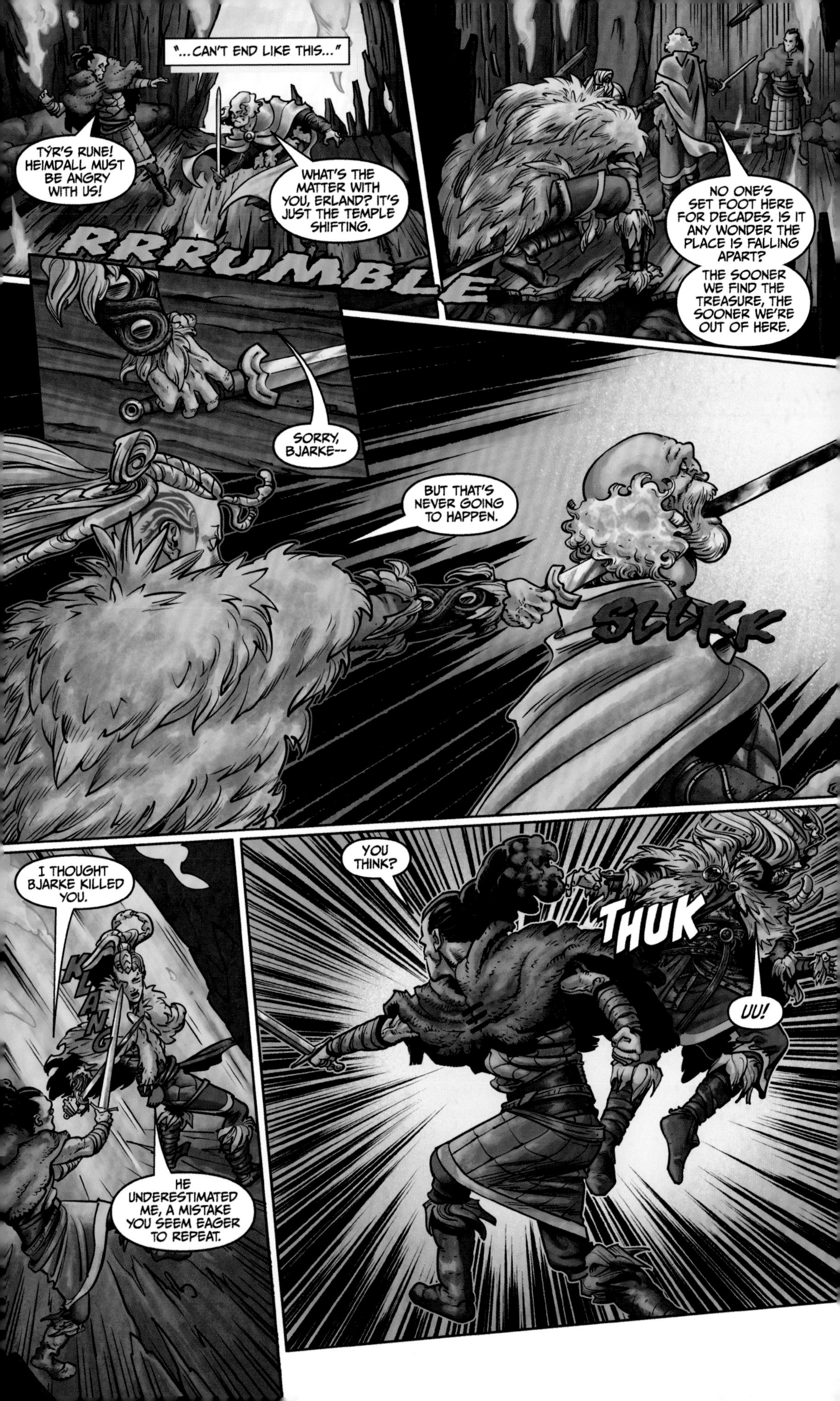
"...CAN'T END LIKE THIS..."
TÝR'S RUNE! HEIMDALL MUST BE ANGRY WITH US!
WHAT'S THE MATTER WITH YOU, ERLAND? IT'S JUST THE TEMPLE SHIFTING.
RRRUMBLE
NO ONE'S SET FOOT HERE FOR DECADES. IS IT ANY WONDER THE PLACE IS FALLING APART?
THE SOONER WE FIND THE TREASURE, THE SOONER WE'RE OUT OF HERE.
SORRY, BJARKE--
BUT THAT'S NEVER GOING TO HAPPEN.
SLUKK
I THOUGHT BJARKE KILLED YOU.
KLANG
HE UNDERESTIMATED ME, A MISTAKE YOU SEEM EAGER TO REPEAT.
YOU THINK?
THUK
UU!

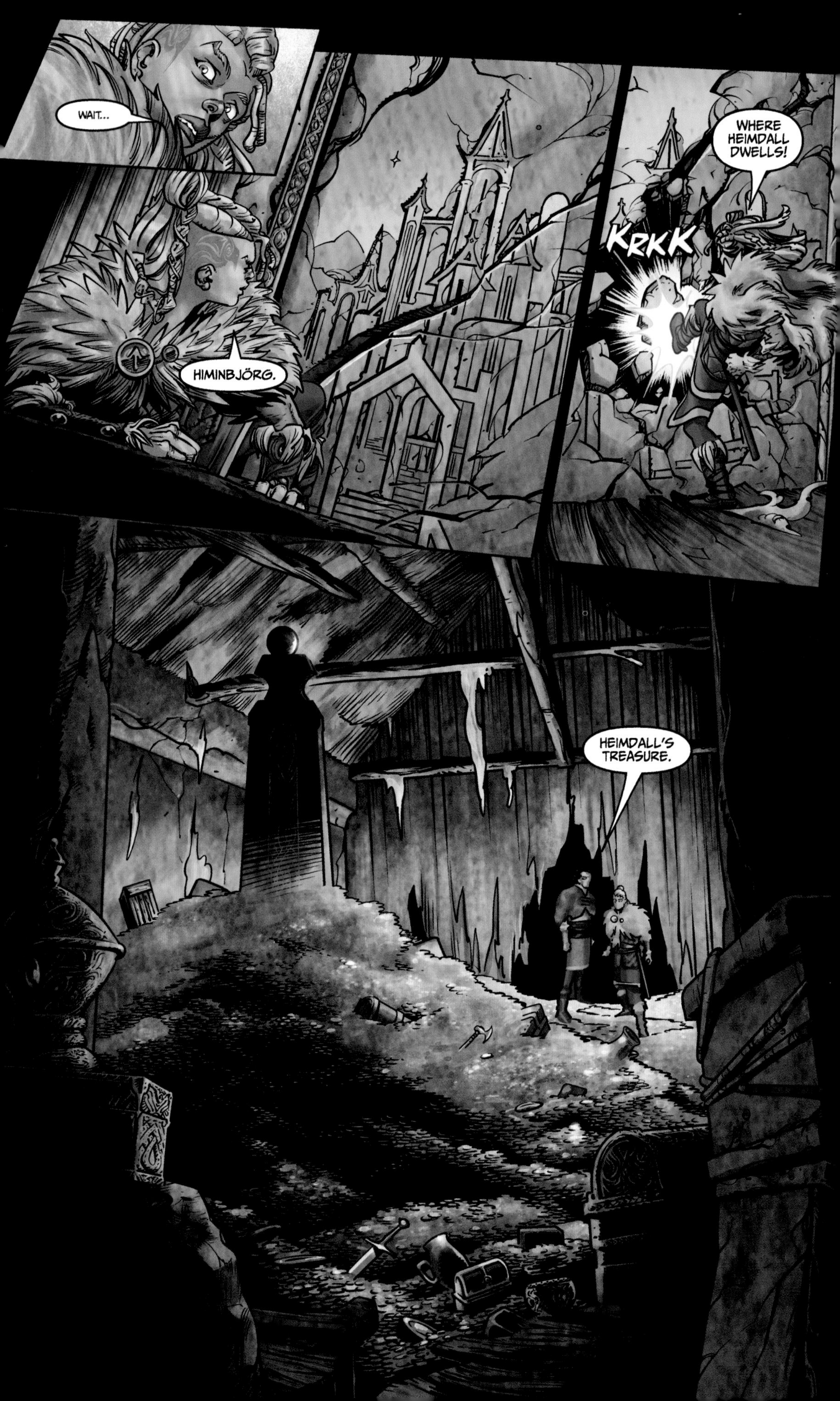
WAIT...
HIMINBJÖRG.
WHERE HEIMDALL DWELLS!
KRKK
HEIMDALL'S TREASURE.

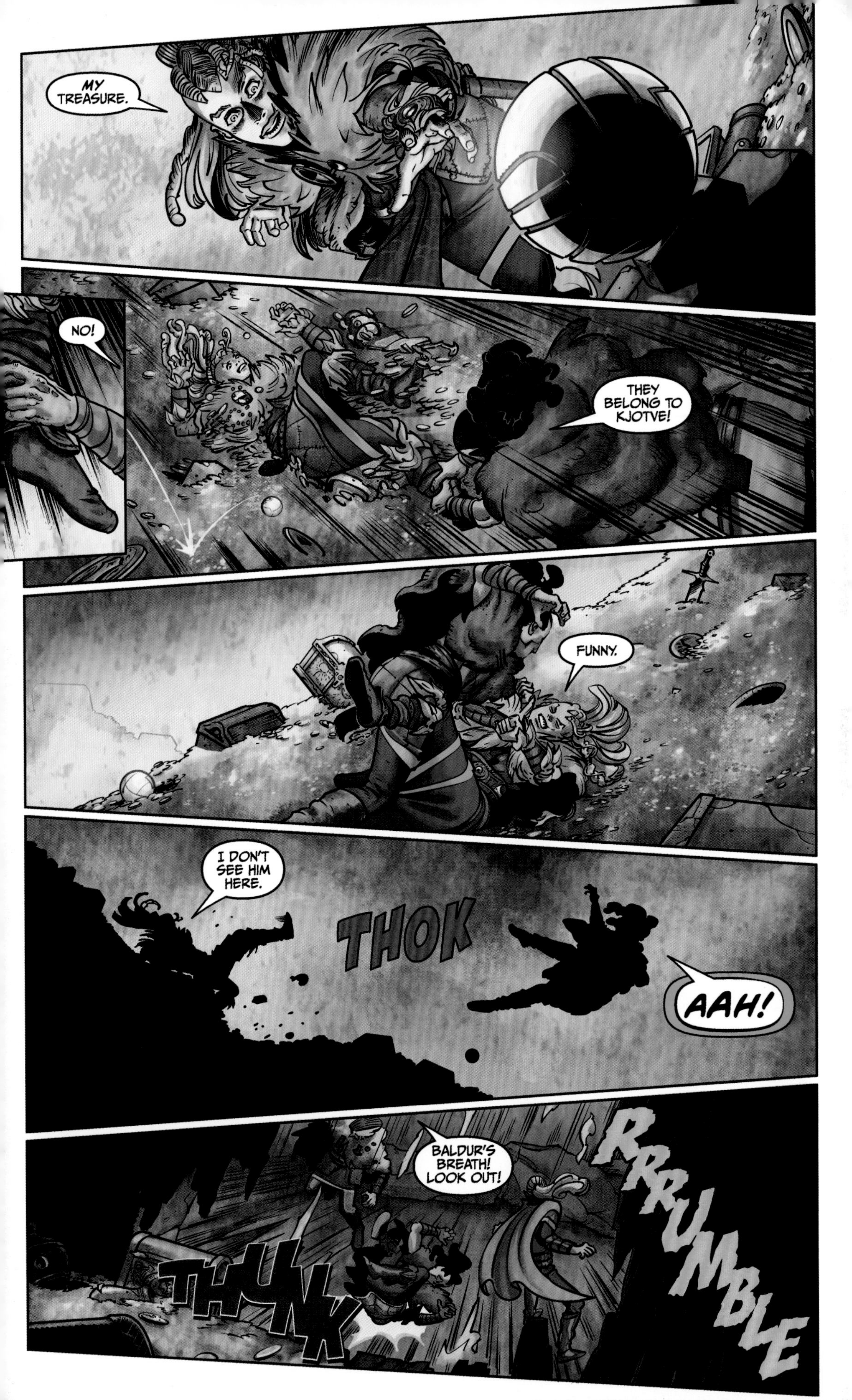
MY TREASURE.
NO!
THEY BELONG TO KJOTVE!
FUNNY.
I DON'T SEE HIM HERE.
THOK
AAH!
BALDUR'S BREATH! LOOK OUT!
RRRUMBLE
THUNK

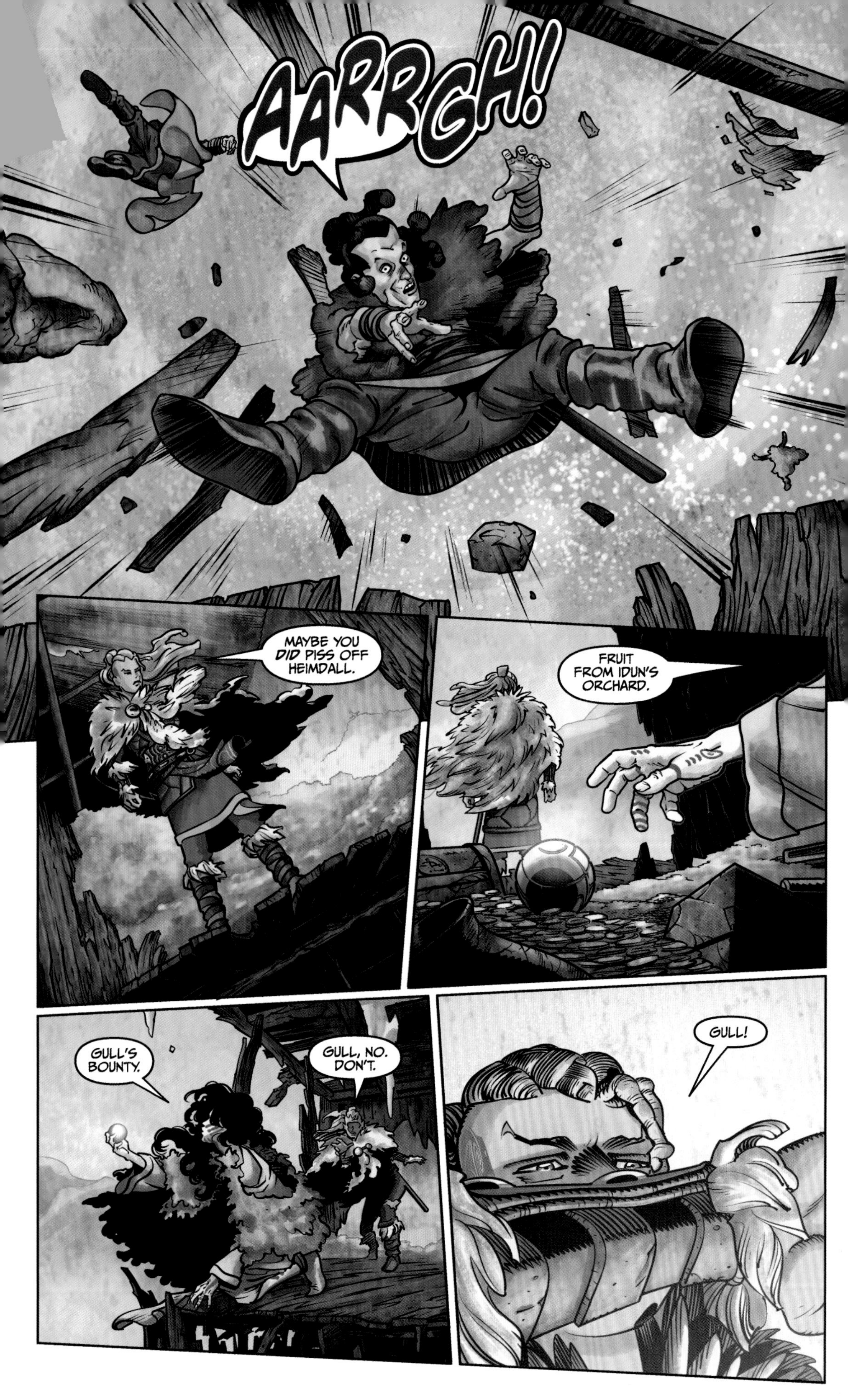
AARRGH!
MAYBE YOU DID PISS OFF HEIMDALL.
FRUIT FROM IDUN'S ORCHARD.
GULL'S BOUNTY.
GULL, NO. DON'T.
GULL!

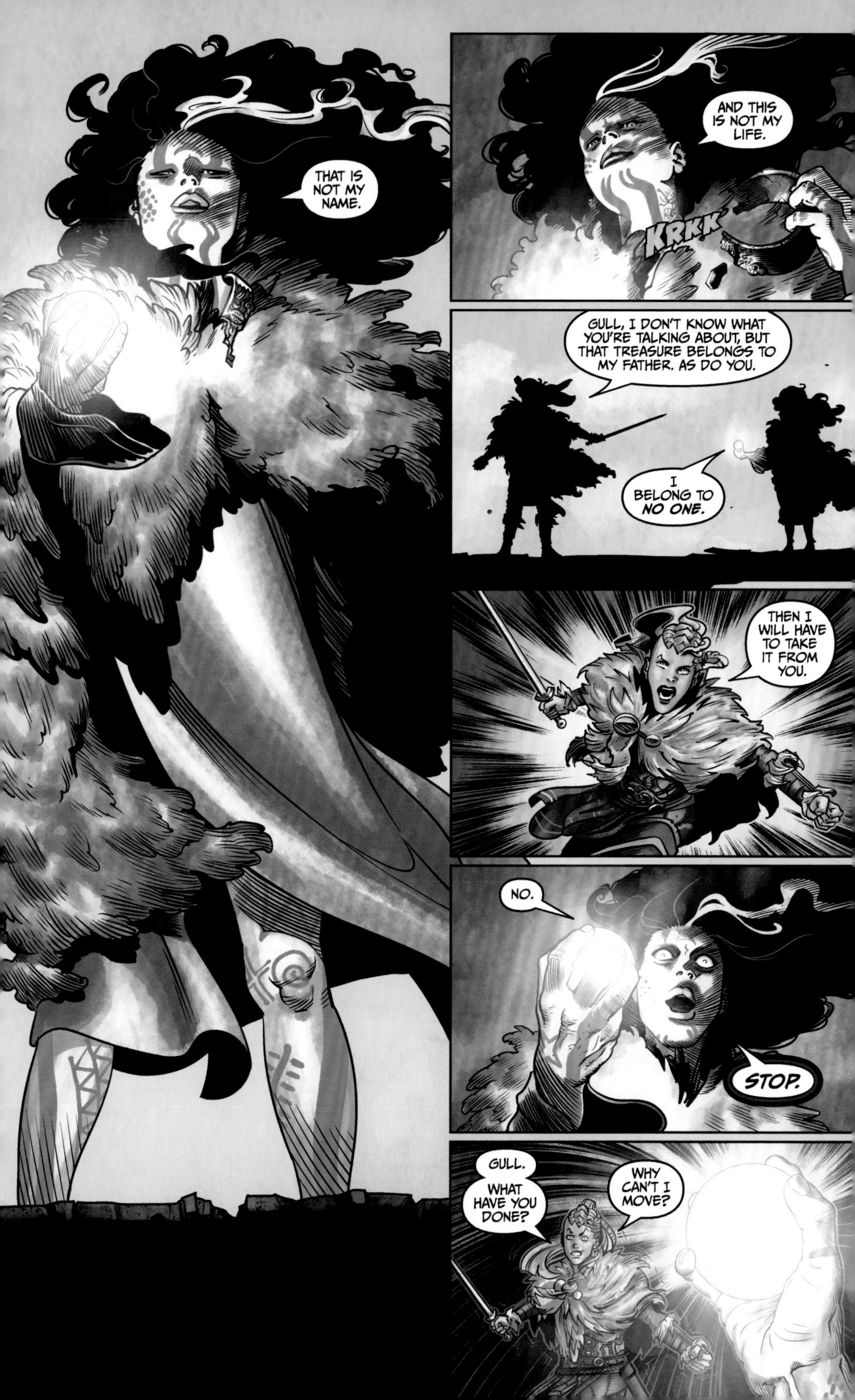
THAT IS NOT MY NAME.
AND THIS IS NOT MY LIFE.
KRKK
GULL, I DON'T KNOW WHAT YOU'RE TALKING ABOUT, BUT THAT TREASURE BELONGS TO MY FATHER. AS DO YOU.
I BELONG TO NO ONE.
THEN I WILL HAVE TO TAKE IT FROM YOU.
NO.
STOP.
GULL.
WHAT HAVE YOU DONE?
WHY CAN'T I MOVE?

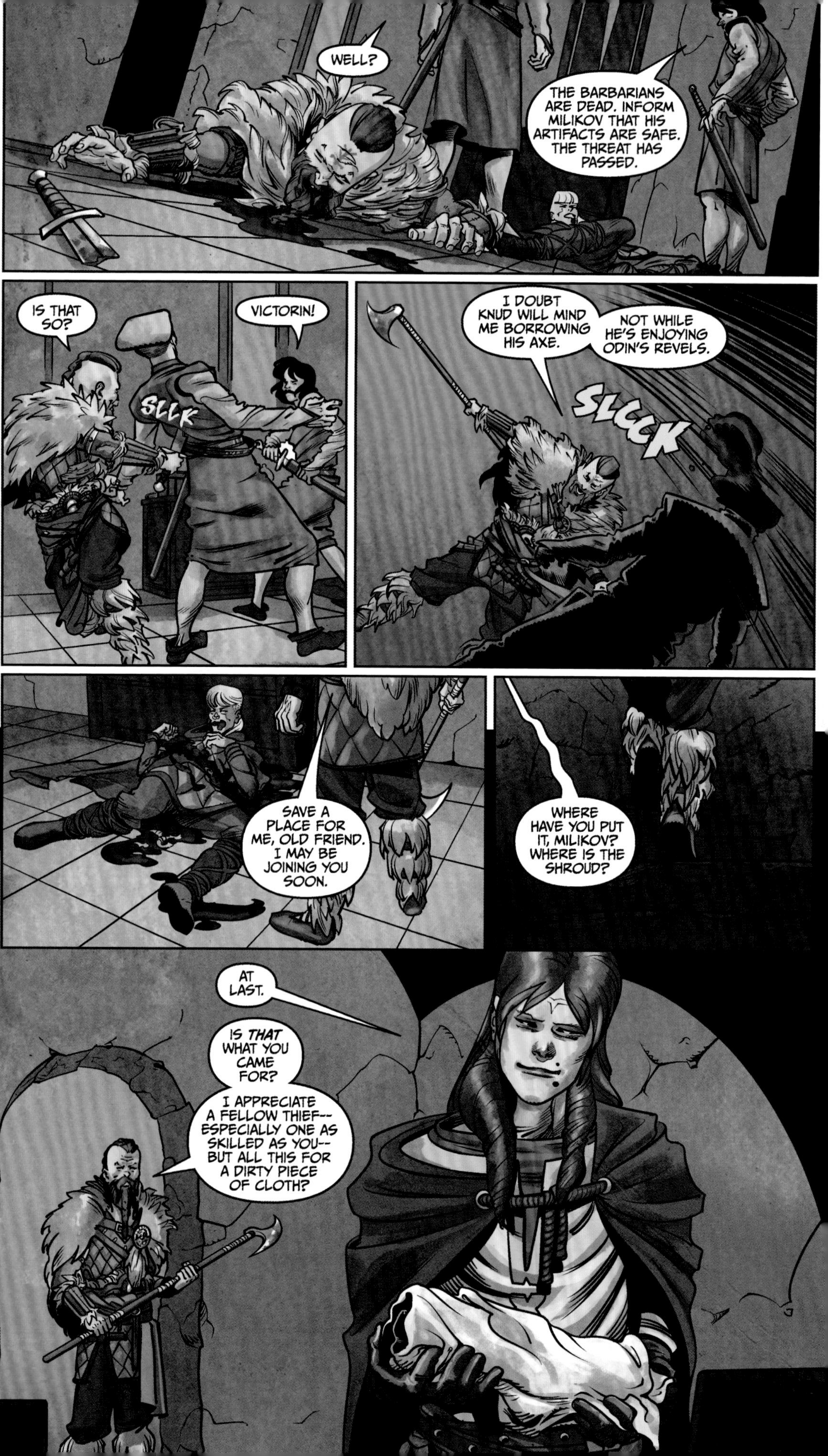

WELL?
THE BARBARIANS ARE DEAD. INFORM MILIKOV THAT HIS ARTIFACTS ARE SAFE. THE THREAT HAS PASSED.
IS THAT SO?
VICTORIN!
SLLK
I DOUBT KNUD WILL MIND ME BORROWING HIS AXE.
NOT WHILE HE'S ENJOYING ODIN'S REVELS.
SLUCK
SAVE A PLACE FOR ME, OLD FRIEND. I MAY BE JOINING YOU SOON.
WHERE HAVE YOU PUT IT, MILIKOV? WHERE IS THE SHROUD?
AT LAST.
IS *THAT* WHAT YOU CAME FOR?
I APPRECIATE A FELLOW THIEF--ESPECIALLY ONE AS SKILLED AS YOU--BUT ALL THIS FOR A DIRTY PIECE OF CLOTH?

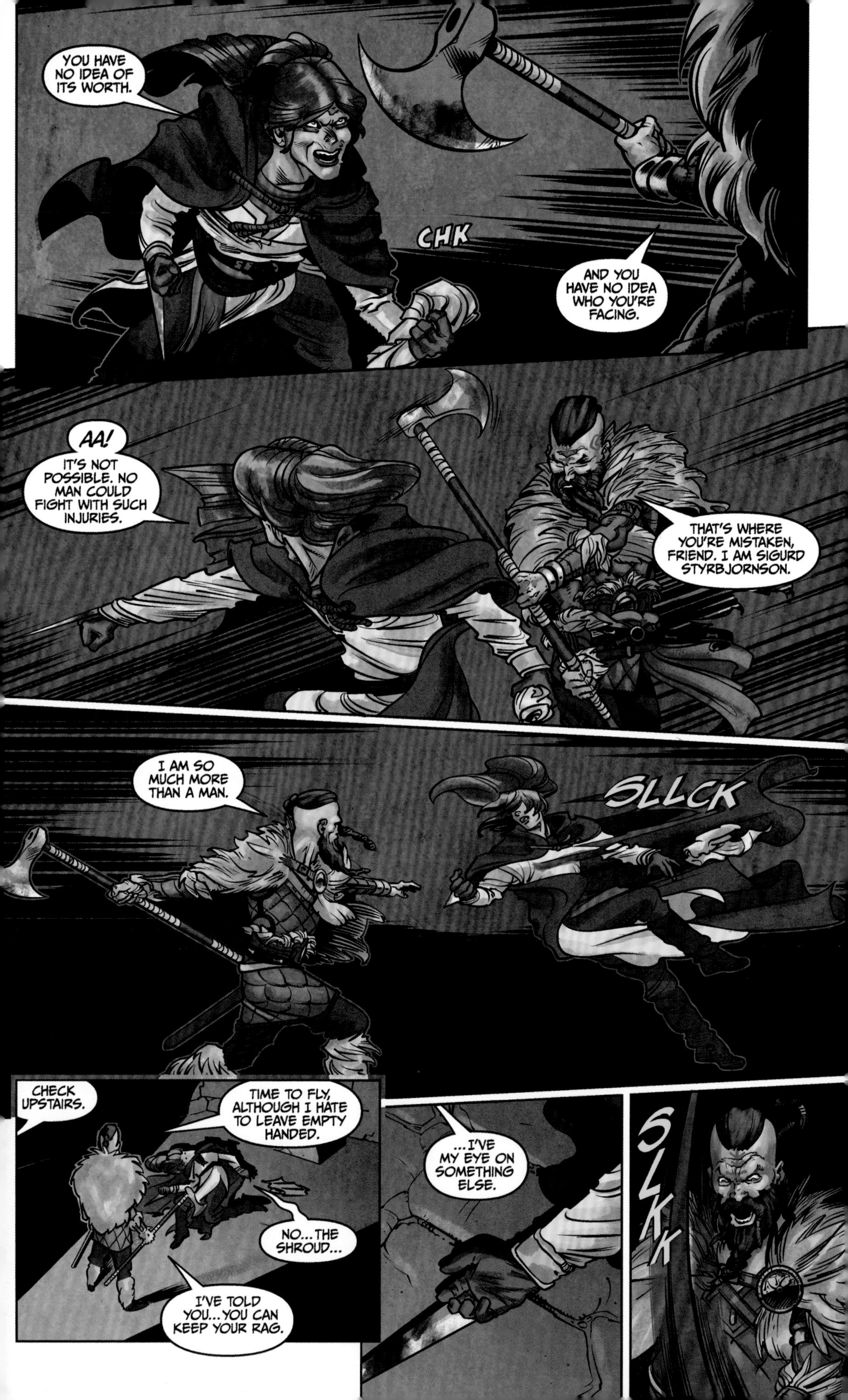
YOU HAVE NO IDEA OF ITS WORTH.
CHK
AND YOU HAVE NO IDEA WHO YOU'RE FACING.
AA!
IT'S NOT POSSIBLE. NO MAN COULD FIGHT WITH SUCH INJURIES.
THAT'S WHERE YOU'RE MISTAKEN, FRIEND. I AM SIGURD STYRBJORNSON.
I AM SO MUCH MORE THAN A MAN.
SLLCK
CHECK UPSTAIRS.
TIME TO FLY, ALTHOUGH I HATE TO LEAVE EMPTY HANDED.
NO... THE SHROUD...
I'VE TOLD YOU... YOU CAN KEEP YOUR RAG.
...I'VE MY EYE ON SOMETHING ELSE.
SLKK

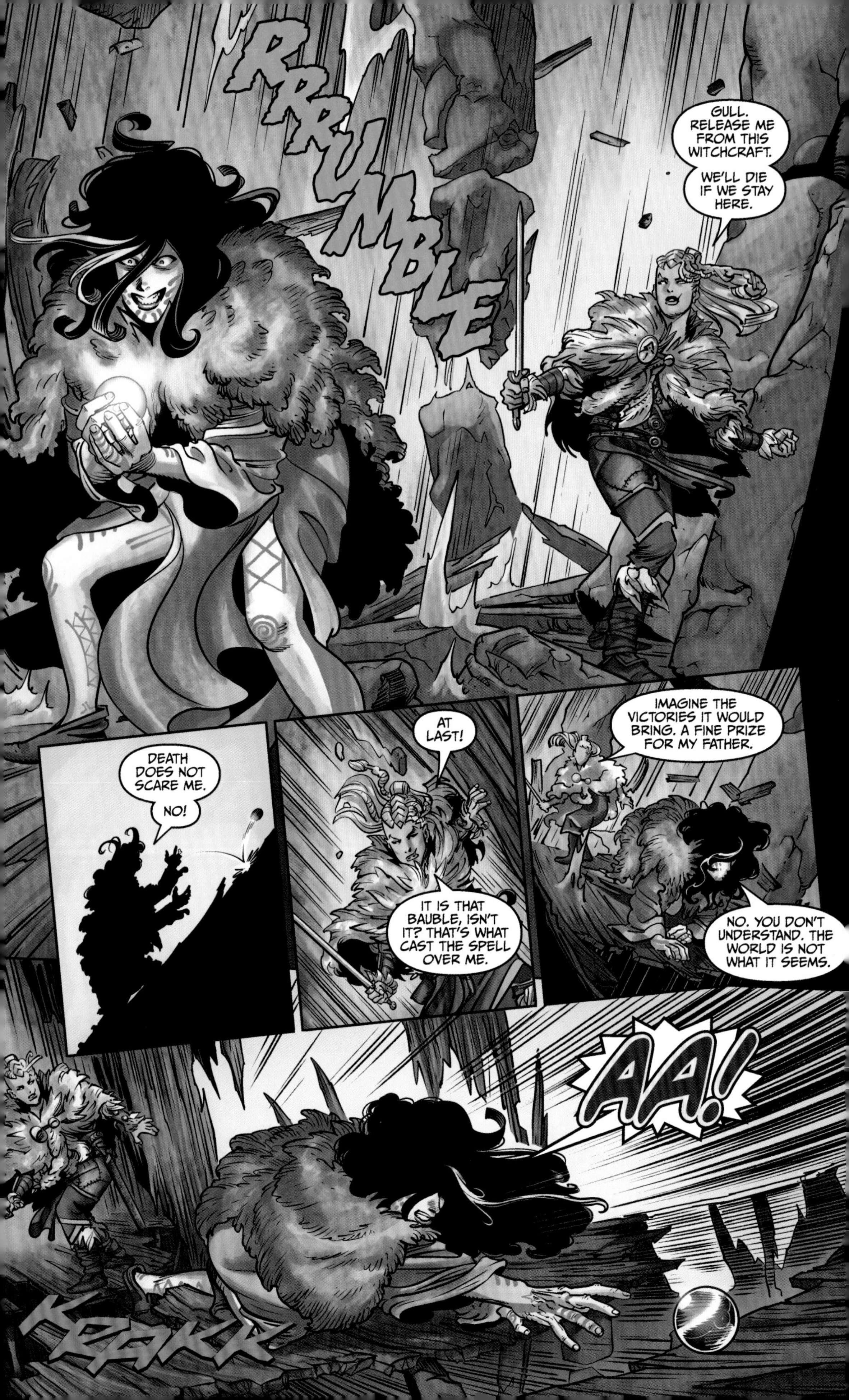
RRRUMBLE
GULL. RELEASE ME FROM THIS WITCHCRAFT.
WE'LL DIE IF WE STAY HERE.
DEATH DOES NOT SCARE ME.
NO!
AT LAST!
IT IS THAT BAUBLE, ISN'T IT? THAT'S WHAT CAST THE SPELL OVER ME.
IMAGINE THE VICTORIES IT WOULD BRING. A FINE PRIZE FOR MY FATHER.
NO. YOU DON'T UNDERSTAND. THE WORLD IS NOT WHAT IT SEEMS.
AA!
KRAKK

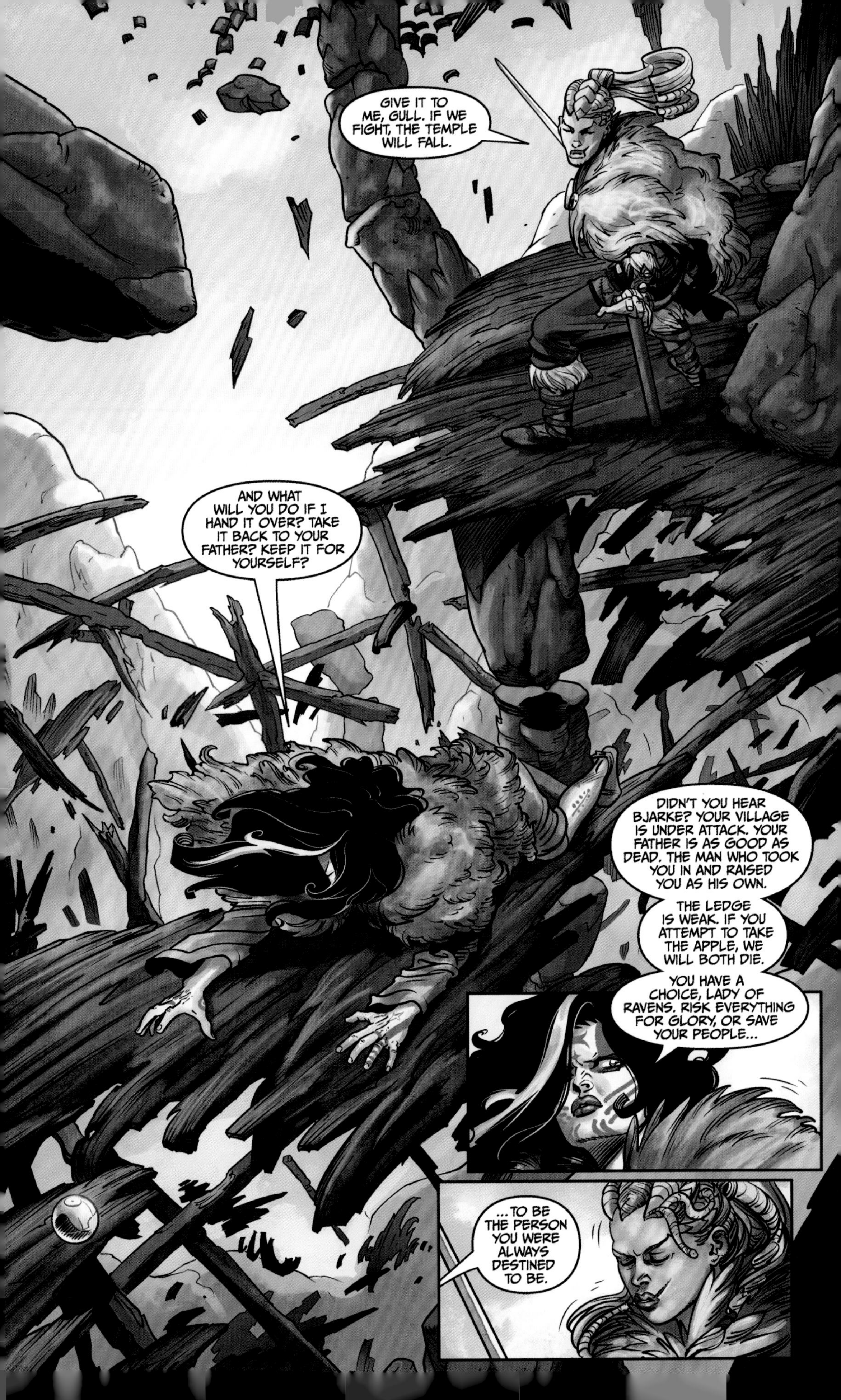
GIVE IT TO ME, GULL. IF WE FIGHT, THE TEMPLE WILL FALL.
AND WHAT WILL YOU DO IF I HAND IT OVER? TAKE IT BACK TO YOUR FATHER? KEEP IT FOR YOURSELF?
DIDN'T YOU HEAR BJARKE? YOUR VILLAGE IS UNDER ATTACK. YOUR FATHER IS AS GOOD AS DEAD. THE MAN WHO TOOK YOU IN AND RAISED YOU AS HIS OWN.
THE LEDGE IS WEAK. IF YOU ATTEMPT TO TAKE THE APPLE, WE WILL BOTH DIE.
YOU HAVE A CHOICE, LADY OF RAVENS. RISK EVERYTHING FOR GLORY, OR SAVE YOUR PEOPLE...
...TO BE THE PERSON YOU WERE ALWAYS DESTINED TO BE.

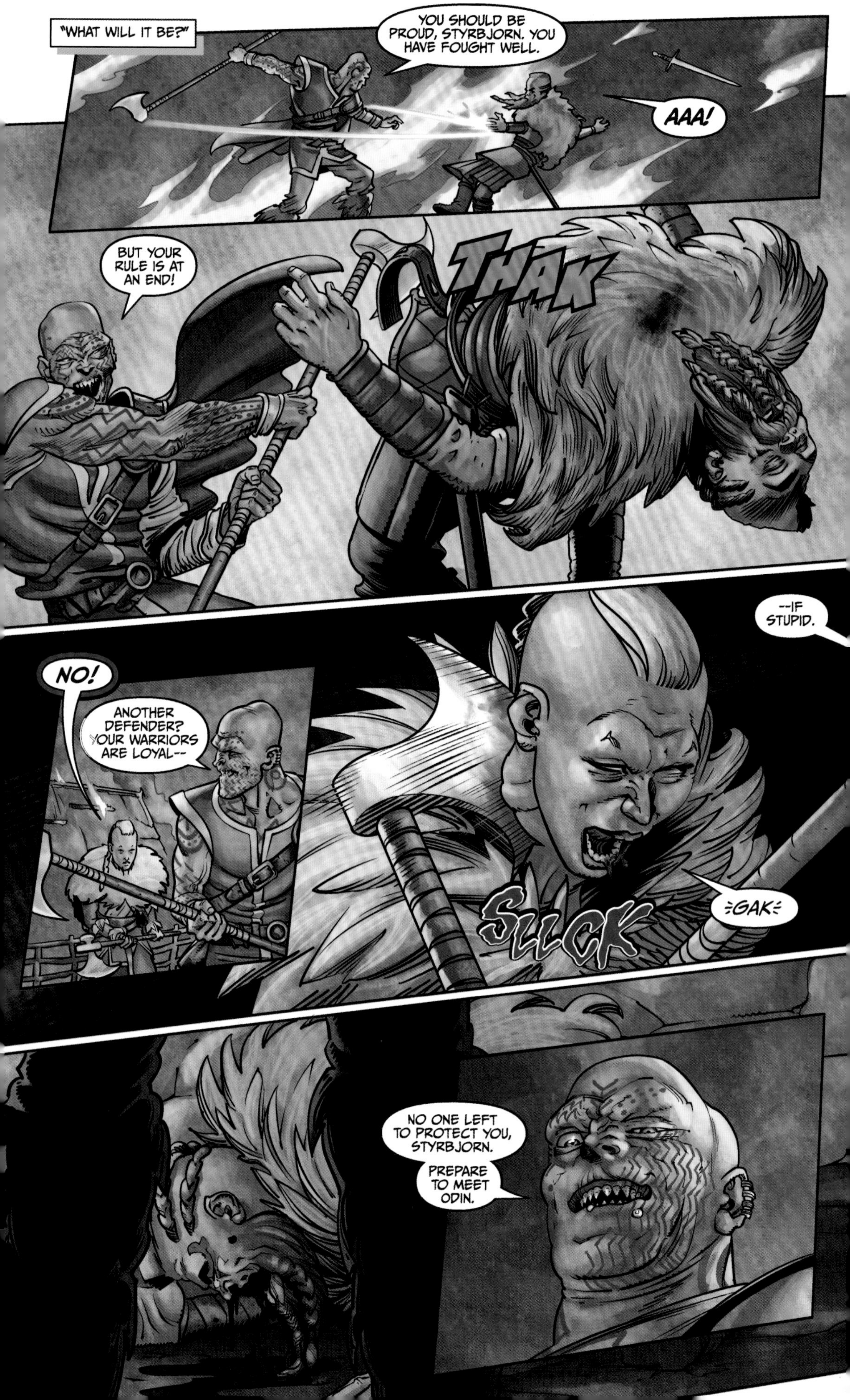
"WHAT WILL IT BE?"
YOU SHOULD BE PROUD, STYRBJORN. YOU HAVE FOUGHT WELL.
AAA!
BUT YOUR RULE IS AT AN END!
THAK
NO!
ANOTHER DEFENDER? YOUR WARRIORS ARE LOYAL--
--IF STUPID.
SLLCK
GAK
NO ONE LEFT TO PROTECT YOU, STYRBJORN.
PREPARE TO MEET ODIN.

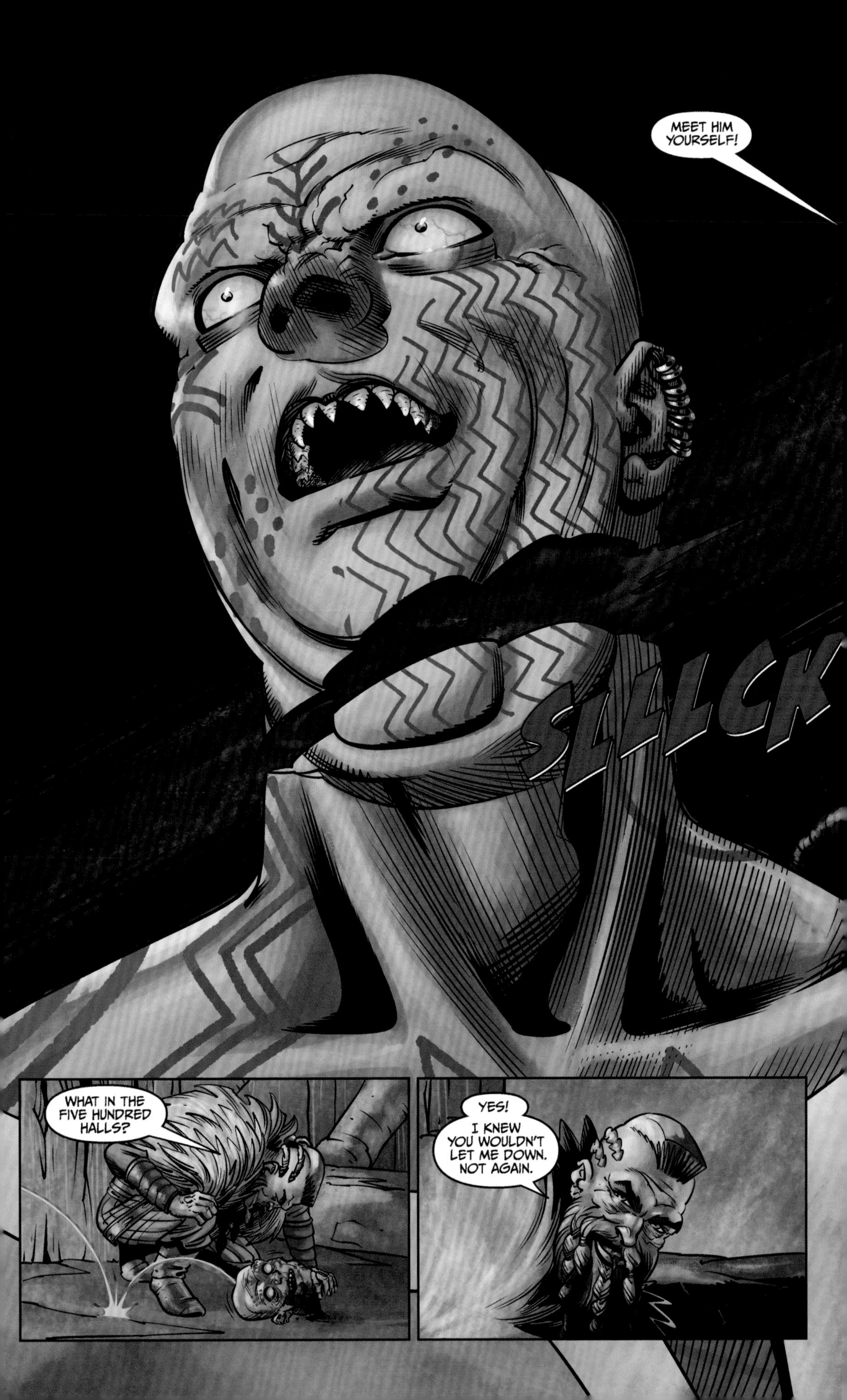
MEET HIM YOURSELF!
SLLLCK
WHAT IN THE FIVE HUNDRED HALLS?
YES!
I KNEW YOU WOULDN'T LET ME DOWN. NOT AGAIN.

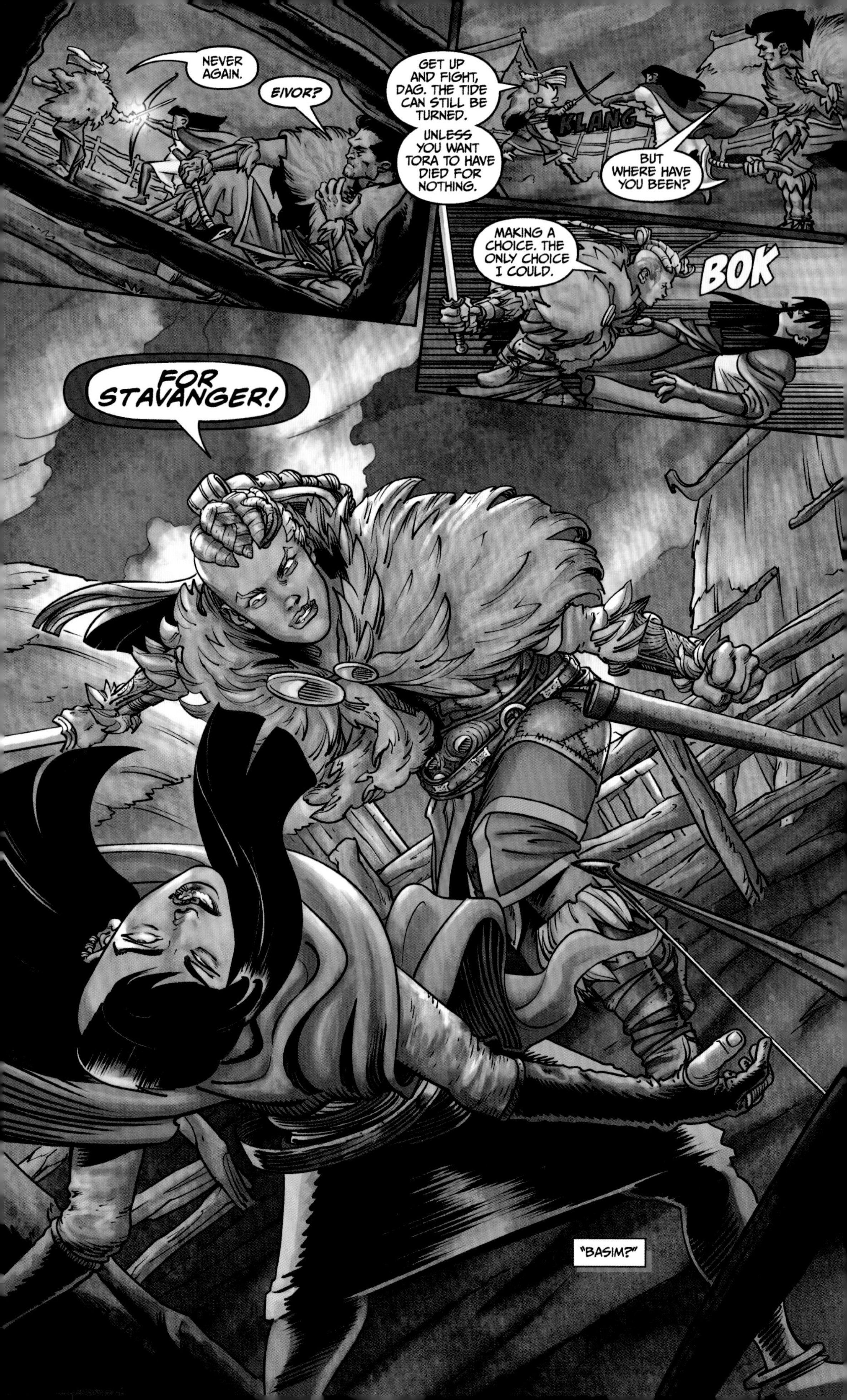
NEVER AGAIN.
EIVOR?
GET UP AND FIGHT, DAG. THE TIDE CAN STILL BE TURNED.
UNLESS YOU WANT TORA TO HAVE DIED FOR NOTHING.
KLANG
BUT WHERE HAVE YOU BEEN?
MAKING A CHOICE. THE ONLY CHOICE I COULD.
BOK
FOR STAVANGER!
"BASIM?"

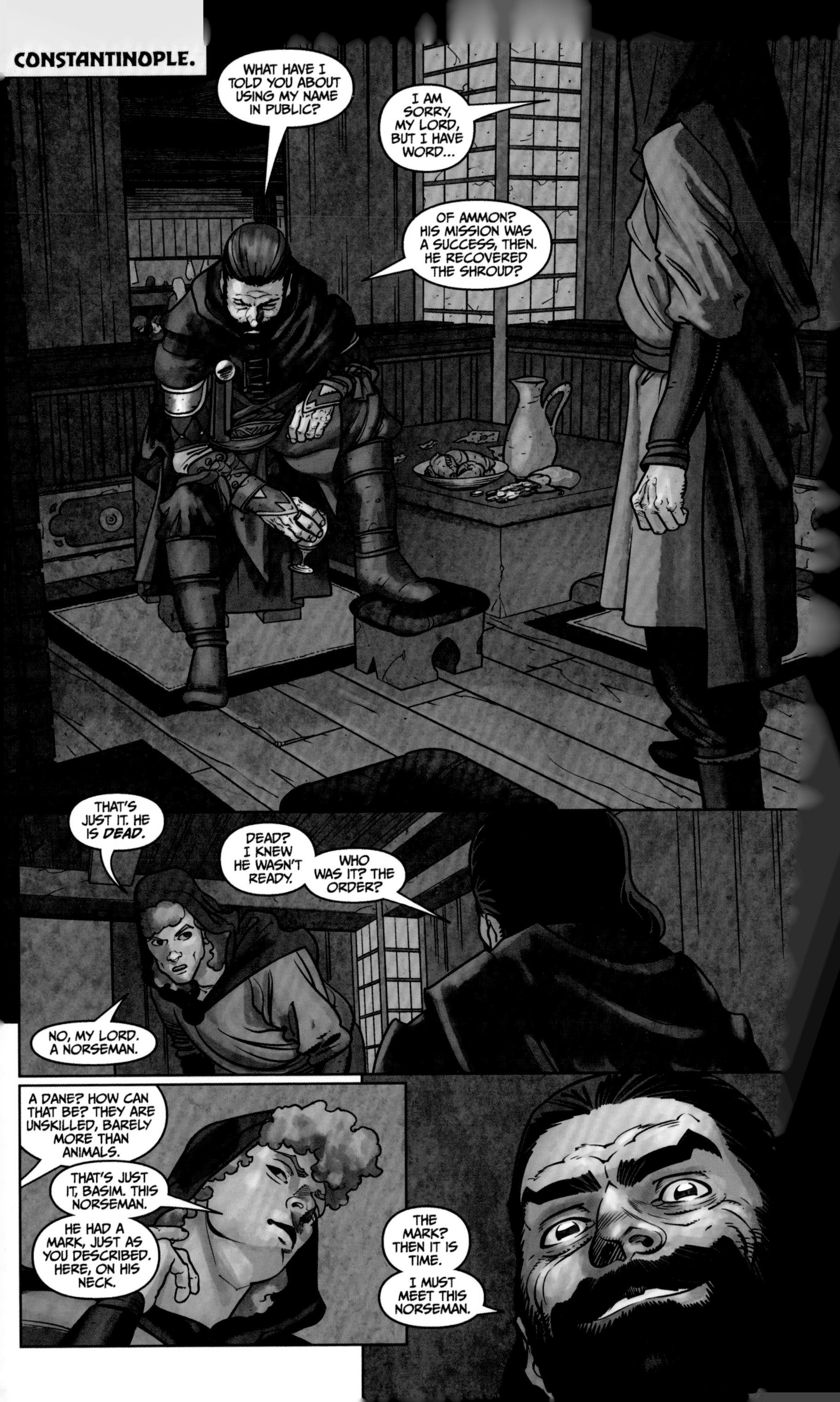
CONSTANTINOPLE.
WHAT HAVE I TOLD YOU ABOUT USING MY NAME IN PUBLIC?
I AM SORRY, MY LORD, BUT I HAVE WORD...
OF AMMON? HIS MISSION WAS A SUCCESS, THEN. HE RECOVERED THE SHROUD?
THAT'S JUST IT. HE IS *DEAD*.
DEAD? I KNEW HE WASN'T READY.
WHO WAS IT? THE ORDER?
NO, MY LORD. A NORSEMAN.
A DANE? HOW CAN THAT BE? THEY ARE UNSKILLED, BARELY MORE THAN ANIMALS.
THAT'S JUST IT, BASIM. THIS NORSEMAN.
HE HAD A MARK, JUST AS YOU DESCRIBED. HERE, ON HIS NECK.
THE MARK? THEN IT IS TIME.
I MUST MEET THIS NORSEMAN.

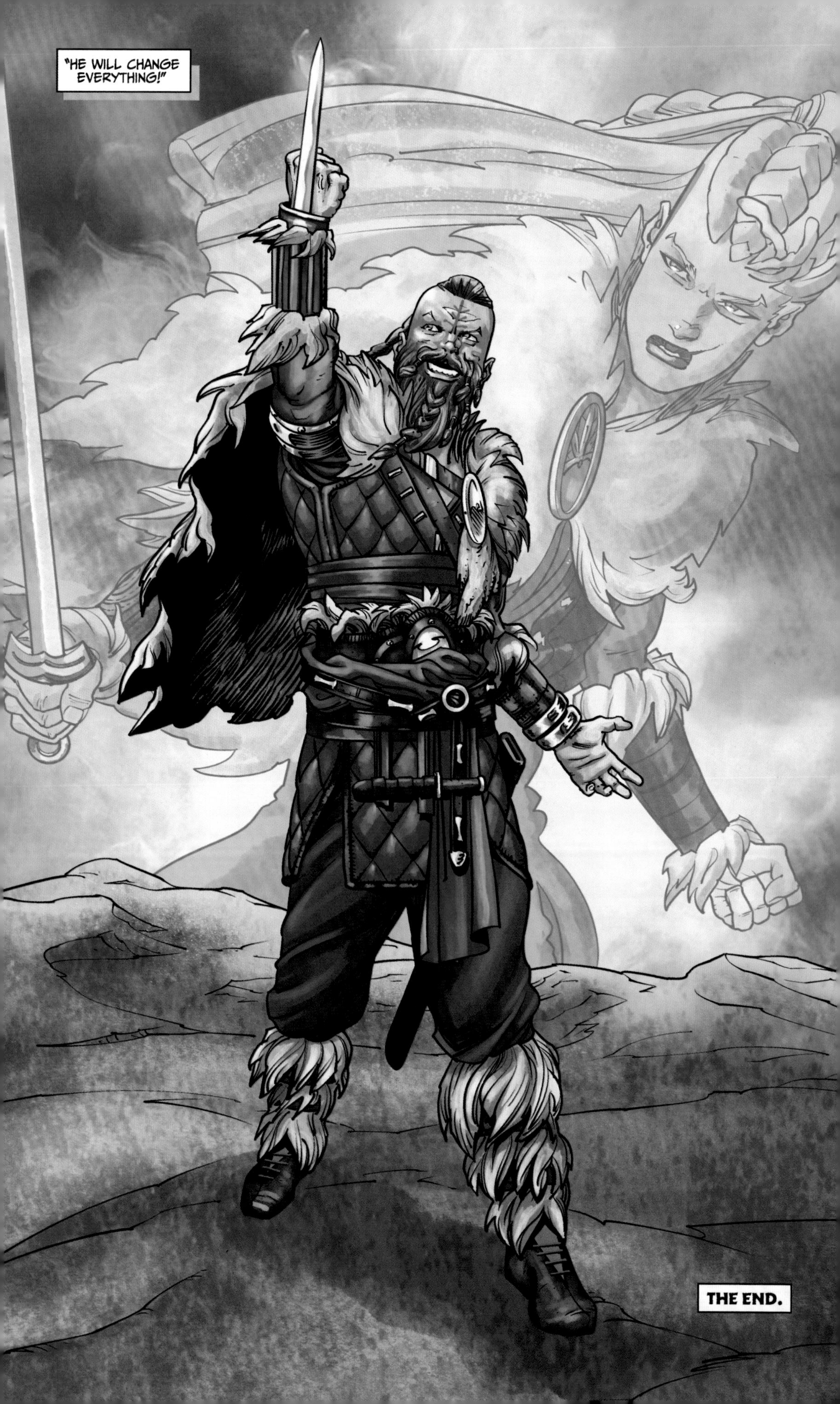
"HE WILL CHANGE EVERYTHING!"
THE END.

A CLOSE LOOK INSIDE THE DEVELOPMENT OF UBISOFT'S *ASSASSIN'S CREED® VALHALLA*

THE ART OF
ASSASSIN'S
CREED
VALHALLA

THE ART OF ASSASSIN'S CREED VALHALLA

This masterfully designed art book offers an insider's look at the immersive art direction of *Assassin's Creed® Valhalla*. Featuring iconic artworks ranging from stunning settings to brutal weapons, as well as developer insights.

978-1-50671-931-3 // $39.99

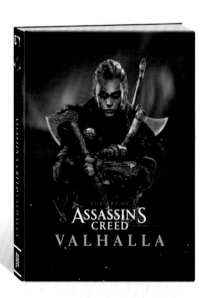

THE ART OF ASSASSIN'S CREED VALHALLA

THE ART OF ASSASSIN'S CREED VALHALLA (DELUXE EDITION)

This deluxe edition includes an exclusive cover, a decorative slipcase, and a gallery-quality lithograph art print.

978-1-50672-045-6 // $79.99

DARK HORSE BOOKS

UBISOFT

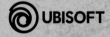

AVAILABLE AT YOUR LOCAL COMICS SHOP OR BOOKSTORE!

To find a comics shop in your area, visit comicshoplocator.com // For more information or to order direct, visit DarkHorse.com

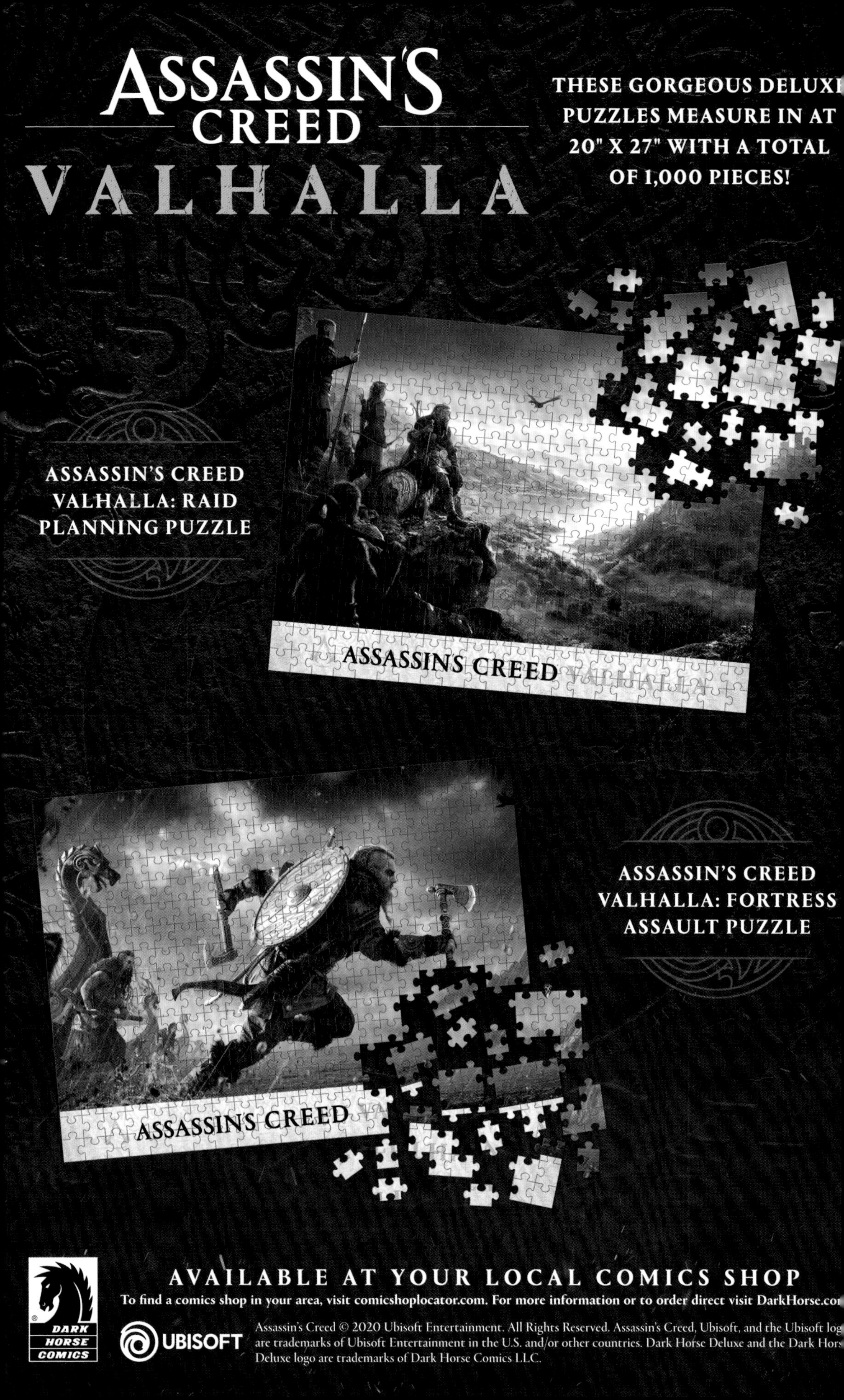

ASSASSIN'S CREED
VALHALLA
THESE GORGEOUS DELUX
PUZZLES MEASURE IN AT
20" X 27" WITH A TOTAL
OF 1,000 PIECES!
ASSASSIN'S CREED
VALHALLA: RAID
PLANNING PUZZLE
ASSASSINS CREED
ASSASSIN'S CREED
VALHALLA: FORTRESS
ASSAULT PUZZLE
ASSASSIN'S CREED
AVAILABLE AT YOUR LOCAL COMICS SHOP
To find a comics shop in your area, visit comicshoplocator.com. For more information or to order direct visit DarkHorse.co
DARK HORSE COMICS
UBISOFT
Assassin's Creed © 2020 Ubisoft Entertainment. All Rights Reserved. Assassin's Creed, Ubisoft, and the Ubisoft log
are trademarks of Ubisoft Entertainment in the U.S. and/or other countries. Dark Horse Deluxe and the Dark Hors
Deluxe logo are trademarks of Dark Horse Comics LLC.